RAVENS FOR
ROUND BOTTOM

CW00517902

RAVENS FORD 0.7
ROUND BOTTOM 12.0

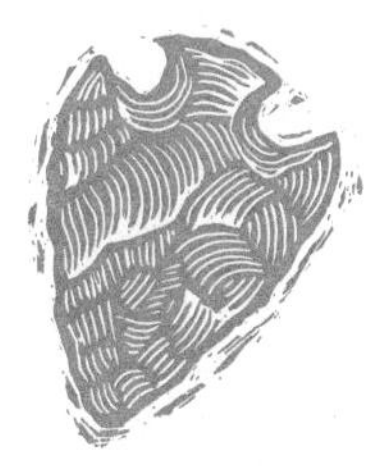

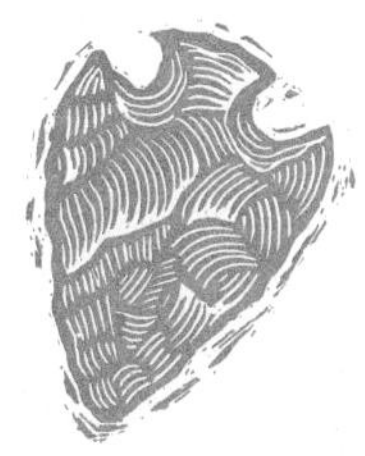

RAVENS FORD 0.7
ROUND BOTTOM 12.0

PLACE NAMES

OF THE SMOKIES

BY
Allen R. Coggins

EDITED BY: Steve Kemp & Kent Cave
DESIGNED BY: Christina Watkins
TYPOGRAPHY & PRODUCTION BY: TypeWorks
PHOTOGRAPHY COURTESY: National Park Service
PROJECT COORDINATION BY: Steve Kemp
EDITORIAL ASSISTANCE BY: Marjorie Kemp, Ruth Richardson, and Marianne Wightman

Printed on recycled paper in the United States of America by Edwards Brothers, Inc.

first edition

1 2 3 4 5 6 7 8 9 10

ISBN 0-937207-23-3

Great Smoky Mountains Natural History Association is a private, nonprofit organization which supports the educational, scientific, and historical programs of Great Smoky Mountains National Park. Our publications are an educational service intended to enhance the public's understanding and enjoyment of the national park. If you would like to know more about our publications, memberships, guided hikes and other projects, please contact: Great Smoky Mountains Natural History Association, 115 Park Headquarters Road, Gatlinburg, TN 37738 (423) 436-7318. www.nps.gov/grsm

This book is lovingly dedicated to my father,
William Lawrence Coggins, Sr.,
whose cremated remains were spread
on Clingmans Dome, within
Great Smoky Mountains National Park,
in the spring of 1992.

CONTENTS

ACKNOWLEDGMENTS

I am greatly indebted to a number of people for their assistance in compiling this book. Annette Hartigan provided invaluable assistance in making the resources of the park library and archives available. I also wish to thank her for her encouragement and suggestions regarding this project. Of course, she had an ulterior motive. As she puts it, "Now when someone asks how a place got its name, it will be easier to find the answer!" I am also grateful to the late Mary Ruth Chiles for her early efforts in compiling some preliminary information on place names in the Smokies. I want to thank my editor, Steve Kemp, for sweating the details and whose intimate knowledge of the book is second only to my own. For access to their books, files, and other records, and for suggestions on other sources, I thank the staffs of both the McClung Historical Collections and the University of Tennessee John C. Hodges Library in Knoxville. I am also appreciative of the following individuals who were interviewed in person, by phone, or who otherwise rendered assistance in locating valuable information: Inez Adams, Glenn Cardwell, Don DeFoe, Voit Gilmore, Kara Gregory, Cheryl Henderson, Royce Jenkins, Clyde Laws, Manard Ledbetter, Kitty Manscill, Jerry McCarter, Sam McCarter, Dwight McCarter, James Ethron Evans, Dr. David A. Etnier, Duane Oliver, Pete Prince, Tom Robbins, Bill Rolen, Bob Shubert, Ron Tagliapietra, Bob Wightman, and Kenneth Wise. I also wish to thank my friends at the JFG Coffee House in Knoxville for providing a marvelous environment in which to write and edit, and for about 4,372 cups of coffee. Finally, I wish to thank my wife Barbara for her love, patience, encouragement, and understanding when I said, "I want to leave something meaningful and useful behind." One of the special moments, early in my journey to complete this book, was when I discovered a Coggins Branch beneath a Cook Knob on the North Carolina side of the park. Cook is my wife's maiden name, and when I showed her the map I said, "Honey, we may be distant (and she added, 'hopefully very distant') cousins."

INTRODUCTION

Who hath not own'd, with rapture-smitten fame,
The power of grace, the magic of a name?
—Thomas Campbell (1777–1844)

Place names are more than mere words used to label points on a map. They are narratives that collectively chronicle the history of an area—be it a nation, county, or small hollow in the southern Appalachian Mountains.

The place names described in this book relate to plants, animals, rocks, topography, and a broad array of historic and prehistoric features. They describe the shape of the land, unusual events, and both celebrated and common people. They relate to agriculture, industry, transportation, and even to the supernatural. Some names are whimsical, some corrupted forms of earlier names, and still others simply unusual, intriguing, or imaginative appellations. All, however, have a common bond. They are tied to a place so special that it is now protected and preserved for the enjoyment of all the people in perpetuity as Great Smoky Mountains National Park.

The meaning of some Smoky Mountain place names, like Chimney Tops, is simple: two rock spires that look like chimneys. Others, like Mellinger Death Ridge, represent more complex stories. One day Jasper Mellinger stumbled into an illegal bear trap on this ridge. When the owners of the trap returned and found Mellinger barely alive from the ordeal, they decided to murder him instead of facing the consequences of their illegal activities. After beating him to death, they disposed of his body in a secluded area. There it lay until one of the perpetrators, on his death bed, confessed to the crime and told where the body could be found. Mellinger's remains were identified by his pocket watch, and the mystery of his disappearance solved after many years.

Still other names, like Injun Creek, can be deceiving. One might assume that this stream was named in a folksy or derogatory manner for a Native American. However, the injun in this case is a steam "engine" that derailed in the 1920s along a stream, formerly called "Indian" Creek.

The origins of still other place names have been lost. Because of the area's isolation, its early history is more oral than written, passing from generation to generation by word of mouth. Some of the old timers had a knack for remembering events and details of the past, including the origins of place names. Unfortunately, once the park came into being, and former occupants moved away, this knowledge base began to wane. Many of its keepers died, and the old and the young lost interest in the oral tradition. How many times have researchers been told, " If only so and so were still alive, she knew everything about the people and the places in the mountains." The adage is true, "When an old person dies, it's like a library burning down." For these reasons, we may never know what some places were called, let alone the meanings of their names.

Multiple place name explanations are not uncommon and in some cases we must resort to educated guesses (based upon credible sources or other clues) to ascertain the meanings of names. For example, if a Hall Cabin is found on a map near a place called the Hall Cemetery, and the cemetery is known to be named for a Hall family that settled in the area, it is probably reasonable to conclude that the cabin was also named for the same Hall family. However, there is the case of Jay Bird Branch. One would assume that the stream was named for the blue jay, a common bird in the park. On the other hand, there is always the possibility that the stream was named for the fact that mountain boys went skinny-dipping in this stream and that the name could relate to the old expression, "naked as a jay bird."

A number of such deceiving names can be cited. For example, the American elk once roamed throughout the southern Appalachians and in the early 1800s could still be found throughout the area that is now the park. However, Elkmont, formerly Elk Mountain, a familiar place name in the Smokies, was not named for this animal. It was named for the large, weekend-long picnics once held here by members of the

Knoxville Elks Club (a men's benevolent and social fraternity). Consequently, where doubt existed, I have modified explanations with "probably," "possibly," or "may be." Otherwise the reader may assume the origin was documented or provided by a reliable, authoritative source or informant.

Several place names have a number of origin theories attached to them. Two good examples are Cades Cove with four or more possible origins and Fighting Creek with at least five. Value judgments on origins have generally been avoided in this work; however, because some sources are more reliable than others, some more plausible theories have occasionally been suggested.

The late Paul M. Fink was one of the first individuals to seriously delve into the origin of Smoky Mountain place names. His 1956, 20-page book on the subject, *That's Why They Call It . . .*, is currently out of print. In this narrative he discussed the meanings of over 130 of the more interesting place names in the park and surrounding area. He also commented on some of the more provocative topographic terms found in the southern Appalachians. Some of his earlier writings were published in the East Tennessee Historical Society: Publications, including "Early Explorers in the Great Smokies" (1933), "Smoky Mountains History as Told in Place-Names" (1934), and "The Nomenclature of the Great Smoky Mountains," which he co-authored with M. H. Avery in 1937. It was from these earlier articles that he drew much of the information for his later book.

The late Hiram C. Wilburn, a historian and folklorist from Waynesville, North Carolina, also worked on an alphabetical listing of Smoky Mountain place name origins in the late 1930s. Popular local or regional authors, like T. H. Alexander, Carson Brewer, John Parris, Vic Weals, and E. V. Sherrick have likewise added to our knowledge of place names through regular or periodic newspaper columns about the Smokies.

The late Mary Ruth Chiles, former secretary to a number of park superintendents, devoted considerable time, both before and after her retirement, to assembling a mini-gazetteer of the park. A number of her original file entries also include information on the origins of place names.

My first task in the course of this project was to identify every place name within the boundaries of the park. This was accomplished using the 28 7.5 minute U.S. Geological Survey topographic maps that cover the 520,000-acre park. Additional place names were taken from archival documents, transcribed interviews, and a 1933 official Nomenclature Map of the Smokies.

A search for name origins was conducted concurrently with name listings. This was accomplished by consulting written records and conducting interviews. Much of the information contained in this book was obtained from the Great Smoky Mountains National Park Library and Archives as well as from the McClung Special Collections and University of Tennessee libraries in Knoxville, Tennessee. Sources include books on the Smokies, applicable county and state histories from Tennessee and North Carolina, maps, vertical file materials, photo captions, transcribed interviews, correspondence, and other documents from the park archives. In addition to primary and secondary written documentation, interviews were conducted with retired and current park employees, local historians, former Smoky Mountain residents, and other knowledgeable people.

In order to keep this volume reasonably priced and accessible, some park place names and locations were not included. However, an unabridged, electronic version of the manuscript is available through the Great Smoky Mountains National Park Library, 107 Park Headquarters Road, Gatlinburg, TN 37738.

Likewise, if you have additional information on place names in the park not included in this volume, please contact Allen Coggins via the publisher at Great Smoky Mountains Natural History Association, 115 Park Headquarters Road, Gatlinburg, TN 37738.

EARLY NOMENCLATURE PROBLEMS

Along with park establishment came the need to deal with redundant place names and those places with more than one name. The Park Service determined early that failing to do this would lead to confusion on the part of park visitors as well as permanent and seasonal staff. As a result of isolation, and a lack of frequent contact or communications, the names that one community chose for its coves, streams, and ridges, were often the same as those used by its neighboring communities. For example, each community had one or more grist mills and one or more Mill Creeks or Mill Branches to prove it. In fact, at one time there were over 35 Mill Creeks in what is now the park. Similar vegetation from one area to another also meant that a number of communities had one or more Laurel Creeks, Laurel Branches, Laurel Coves, Laurel Falls or Laurel Gaps. The abundance of river cane gave rise to a number of Cane Creeks, Cane Gaps, Cane Ridges, or Caney Creeks. Other words frequently duplicated in place names included bear, bald, balsam, beech, hickory, Indian, pine, little, big, spruce, still (as in moonshine still), sugar (as in sugar maple), lower, and upper.

Another problem encountered in the early days of the park was duplicate names. Some places were known by as many as 15 different names! Many names originated from the shape or appearance of the topographic feature. Looking up at the main crest of the Great Smoky Mountains from the Tennessee side, a peak might look like one thing. From the North Carolina side, it looked like something entirely different. There being little daily communications between the people on both sides of the mountain and little need for a standard or single name, the dual names remained. Furthermore, being steeped in history, it would be a difficult task to convince people on either side of the state line to give up their pet names for the common good. The area we now call Mount Cammerer is a good example. Tennesseans once called it White Rock for a band of rock covered with gray lichens near its summit. North Carolinians called it Sharp Top for its shape. What were the park visitors, coming from across the country and around world to call it? Official nomenclature committees suggested a third, more neutral name, Mount Cammerer, in honor of Arno B. Cammerer, a former Director of the National Park Service and a strong advocate for the park.

NOMENCLATURE COMMITTEES

To deal with these problems of redundant and dual place names, the National Park Service and the U.S. Board of Geographic Names requested that a nomenclature committee be established in each state. Since government officials knew that renaming places would be a political challenge as well as a logistical one, the states were asked to choose their committees carefully. They needed to appoint a few strong individuals who could work with each other and with their sister committees to solve common problems—people of strong will, imagination, and integrity.

One of the biggest dilemmas would be to standardize the names of the peaks along the state line ridge that had duplicate names and to label prominent peaks as yet unnamed. There would be a need to dedicate and name some places for prominent individuals who had been active in the establishment of a national park in the Smokies, but there was also a long-standing policy by the U.S. Board of Geographic Names and the National Park Service of not naming topographic features for living individuals. In fact, the nomenclature committees adopted a set of guiding principles regarding their actions. In their own words, "We are opposed to changing the name of any feature of the park unless the name is so confusing . . . as to need changing regardless of any other consideration. We recognize the desirability of descriptive or picturesque names if they really fit the feature to which they are attached, but we also recognize the appropriateness of naming the features in honor of people who did outstanding work for the region in question, and that much history is thus recorded." The committee and the park did, however, have the option of naming roads, trails, bridges, overlooks, and other such features for living VIPs.

Each state appointed its own committee to study the problems and come up with recommendations that were submitted to the United States Board of Geographic Names. This board's task was to consider the proposals and accept or reject them on a case by case basis. This work was to be addressed in two phases. Initial nomenclature committees completed their studies and made their recommendations by 1933 and then disbanded. New committees, composed of different people, were formed in the 1940s to review progress and make further recommendations. Many of the name changes recommended by the early and later nomenclature committees were accepted by the U. S. Board of Geographic Names. Unfortunately, others were not, thus adding to the problem of name redundancy.

Many acres were also added to the park after the nomenclature committees had completed their tasks. For example, the Tennessee Valley Authority acquired some 44,000 acres along the southeast boundary of the park in the early 1940s and subsequently transferred all of it to the park. This was land acquired for the war-time Fontana Dam project. Also since 1945, over 60 additional parcels of land have been added to the park. The largest was a 1,600 acre Aluminum Company of America tract. A majority of the over 100 duplicate names identified in the park today are the result of these later land acquisitions. I have distinguished between the duplicate names by assigning arbitrary numbers to each. For example, the reader will notice that there are two Bearwallow Branches.

NATIVE AMERICAN INFLUENCE ON PLACE NAMES

Considering the long history of the Cherokee in the Smokies, one might expect to find numerous Indian names associated with the park. However, only 6 percent of the place names are related in any way to Native Americans. Furthermore, many of these are not Cherokee terms, but rather general references such as Indian Cove Branch or Red Man Creek. Almost all of the remaining Cherokee language place names have long been anglicized, or otherwise corrupted by whites. This process, the study of which is called folk-etymology, is a common practice for invading cultures. A majority of the early settlers neither understood nor appreciated Native American languages or culture. Theirs was a mission to subdue the wilderness, along with its aboriginal inhabitants. The Indian vernacular was easily misunderstood and mispronounced and with so few written accounts (and until 1821, no written Cherokee language) many of the original words, along with their meanings, have been lost.

Unlike the white settlers who took pride in eventually naming almost everything in their domain, the Cherokee applied place names sparingly. They named places they frequented and conceived of as entities. They labeled their holy places, landmarks important to their limited travels, tribal or community boundaries, their permanent towns, and places in which notable events occurred. The Indians did not usually have names for mountain ranges or even individual large mountains, since these objects were too large to be perceived as entities.

Clingmans Dome, significant to us today as the highest point in the park, was also significant to the Cherokee, but for a different reason. To them it was Kuwahi, the Mulberry Place, where the mystical White Bear had his home. Gregory Bald, some 29 miles to the west, was called Tsistugi. This was the Rabbit Place, home of Little Rabbit, chief of their clan. Mount Le Conte, the third highest peak in the park, was called Walasiyi , and was said to be the home of the giant, mystical green frog. Another source puts the Frog Place at Buckeye Gap. Perhaps there was more than one Frog Place or the true location is questionable.

Cheoah and Chilhowee, now the names of Tennessee Valley Authority lakes, were once the Otter Place and the Valley of the Deer, respectively. Heintooga is the name of a ridge, a bald, a road, and an overlook in a section of the Smokies east of the Qualla Indian Reservation. This place name is a corruption of the Cherokee term Iyentooga, meaning hiding place or refuge. It refers to the vast, wild area visible from the overlook that was literally the last refuge of the Cherokees. Here they resisted banishment from their homeland and the move westward in the 1830s along the infamous Trail of Tears.

Several places are named for Cherokee leaders such as Juney Whank Falls, for Chief Junaluska; Kalanu Prong, for a

Cherokee chief that lived around the time of the American Revolution; and Abrams Falls, for Abram or Old Abraham, a chief of mixed white and Indian blood.

Cataloochee is one of several forms of the Cherokee word Gadalutsi, which loosely translates to fringe standing erect, or standing in ranks, in reference to trees, in a row, along narrow ridges. Both the Oconaluftee River and Ekaneetlee Gap are named for corruptions of the word Egwanulti, meaning all towns along the river.

Some Indian-sounding terms are not of Cherokee origin. The Appalachian Mountains, for example, are named for the Applachees, a tribe of Native Americans that Hernando de Soto found living along the Gulf of Mexico around 1540. Tuskee Gap is short for Tuskegee, a Creek Indian term for warriors. Moccasin, as in Moccasin Branch, is an Algonquian (Narragansett) word for a heelless slipper made of soft, flexible leather. Still other place names like Tomahawk Prong and Big Medicine Creek celebrate the spirit of the Native Americans who once held dominion over the Eastern lands.

The names later applied to places in the Smokies by white explorers and settlers reflected a new ethnocentric terminology based upon entirely different values, experiences, perceptions, dreams, and interpretations.

The place is dignified by the doer's deed.

—William Shakespeare

HOW PLACE NAMES ARE LISTED IN THIS BOOK

Unless otherwise indicated below, place names are listed alphabetically. They are followed by the name and the section of one of the topographic maps on which they are located. Imagine a topographic map divided into nine quadrants which are, from the upper left hand corner clockwise, northwest, north, northeast, east, southeast, south, southwest, and west. The ninth quadrant is located in the center of the map, and is designated M for middle. (See the list of abbreviations at the end of this section.) For example, if a location is **Clingmans Dome** NC/TN se,

Clingmans Dome is the quad name followed by the abbreviations of the two states, North Carolina and Tennessee, in which the quad falls. The "se" means that the place name is located in the southeast quadrant of this map. Some place names, such as streams or roads may cross more than one quad map and/or more than one quadrant in each. For example, the location for **Abrams Creek** is Cades Cove, TN/NC ne-n-nw. The lower case letters, ***n.l.*** and ***n.s.*** are used to designate places "not listed" (feature shown, but no name appears on map) and "not shown" (neither feature nor name appears), on the 28 USGS topographic maps that cover the park.

Where a place name has multiple possible origins, each is listed and numbered.

With the exceptions of some cemeteries and structures, the place names in this book are listed as they appear on the topographic maps and in other park literature. For example, if you are looking for the origin of the place name Kelly Bennett Peak, you'll find it listed in the K's (Kelly Bennett Peak) and not in the B's (Bennett, Kelly Peak). An exception occurs when the word "The" precedes a name as in The Sawteeth or The Sinks. In these cases, the listings read Sawteeth, The and Sinks, The.

U.S.G.S. TOPO MAP DIVIDED INTO QUADRANTS

nw	**n**	**ne**
w	**m**	**e**
sw	**s**	**se**

e	East quadrant	nw	Northwest quadrant
m	Central quadrant	s	South quadrant
n	North quadrant	se	Southeast quadrant
n.l.	Not listed	sw	Southwest quadrant
n.s.	Not shown	TN	Tennessee
NC	North Carolina	w	West quadrant
ne	Northeast quadrant		

U.S.G.S. TOPO MAPS FOR THE GREAT SMOKY MOUNTAINS

Tapoco TVA 1940	Calderwood 1964	Blockhouse TVA 1941–66	
Fontana Dam 1964	Cades Cove 1964	Kinzel Springs TVA 1940–53	
Tuskeegee TVA 1940–61	Thunderhead Mtn. 1964	Wear Cove TVA 1941–53	Walden Creek TVA 1940–53
Noland Creek TVA 1940–61	Silers Bald 1964	Gatlinburg 1930–56	Pigeon Forge 1940–56
Bryson City TVA 1940–60	Clingmans Dome 1964	Mt. Le Conte 1964	Richardson Cove TVA 1940
Whittier TVA 1940–67	Smokemont 1964	Mt. Guyot 1964	Jones Cove TVA 1940
	Bunches Bald 1964	Luftee Knob 1964	Hartford TVA 1940–(68 PR)
	Dellwood TVA 1941	Cove Creek Gap TVA 1941–67	Waterville TVA 1940–(68 PR)

ALPHABETICAL LISTING

PLACE NAMES

OF THE SMOKIES

Abrams Falls

Abrams Creek Cades Cove, TN/NC ne-n-nw **Abrams Falls** Calderwood, TN/NC ne **Abrams Gap** Calderwood, TN/NC w **Abrams Ridge** Calderwood, TN/NC nw-n ❧ Named for Old Abram (Abraham), a Cherokee chief of mixed white and Native American blood whose Chilhowee Village once stood along his namesake creek, west of Cades Cove. He was also known as Ooskuah to the Cherokee.

Ace Creek Smokemont, NC ne-e **Ace Enloe Ridge** Smokemont, NC ne ❧ Named for Ace Enloe, whose family settled in the Oconaluftee area circa 1803. Ace lived at nearby Big Cove and had a tub mill on Ace Creek. He was the grandson of an Abraham Enloe.

Ace Gap Kinzel Springs, TN m ❧ Reported to have been named for the card games once secretly played at this gap by nearby Little River Lumber Company loggers.

Aden Branch Clingmans Dome, NC/TN ne ❧ Probably named for Aden Carter, a resident of this area prior to park establishment.

Aden Carter

Advalorem Branch Noland Creek, NC nw-n ❧ The term Advalorem means a tax based on a percentage of assessed value. This name may therefore relate to some kind of early tax on this property.

Agana Branch Gatlinburg, TN m ❧ Agana is Cherokee for groundhog.

Albright Grove Mt. Guyot, TN/NC ne ***n.s.*** ❧ This is a prominent stand of virgin forest named for Horace Albright, the second director of the National Park Service. Albright was an attorney, but more importantly, he was a conservationist, and a man who advocated that national parks be spread all across the country to preserve and interpret natural and cultural features and serve people. He was a staunch supporter of Great Smoky Mountains National Park and once described it as the most gorgeous of them all. He was also the man most responsible for convincing his close friend, John D. Rockefeller, Jr., to match state, local, and private acquisition funds for the park. See also Rockefeller Memorial.

Allison Branch Bunches Bald, NC ne ***n.s.*** ❧ Named for Joshua Allison, first white settler in Haywood County, North Carolina.

Allnight Ridge Cades Cove, TN/NC ne ❧ So named because a party of hunters once got lost on this ridge and had to wait until daylight to find their way home.

Alum Cave Mt. Le Conte, TN/NC s **Alum Cave Creek** Mt. Le Conte, TN/NC s **Alum Gap** Mt. Le Conte, TN/NC se ❧ This overhanging cliff (not a true cave) is named for the presence of minerals once referred to as alums, but now called pseudo-alums. These mineral salts have formed deposits as water has seeped from and evaporated on the face of the rocks. Miners removed alum, epsom salts, saltpeter, and perhaps other minerals beginning in the 1830s and again during the Civil War. In the 19th century alum was used to dye

Alum Cave

clothes reddish-brown and as a medicine to stop external bleeding. Saltpeter is used to make gunpowder. Recently, some rare (but not particularly valuable) minerals have been discovered at the site. See also Indian Gap and Mount Mingus.

Anakeesta Knob, Anakeesta Ridge Mt. Le Conte, TN/NC s-se ❥ This name, in the Cherokee language, means "place of the balsams." The balsam fir (*Abies balsamea*) is a fragrant evergreen found in the northern Appalachians. It is a close relative of the Fraser fir (*Abies fraseri*) which is found at the high elevations of the southern Appalachians, including the park. Anakeesta is also the name of one of the major rock formations that make up the bulk of the crest of the Great Smoky Mountains.

Andreas Branch Bryson City, NC nw ❧ See Andrews Bald.

Andrews Bald Clingmans Dome, NC/TN sw-w ❧ 1. Named for Andres (Andreas) Thompson, who herded cattle on this bald (see glossary for term bald) in the 1840s. First called Andres (or Anders) Bald but the name was corrupted to Andrews Bald. 2. Named for an Andres (or Anders) family that once ranged their livestock on the bald.

Andy Branch Cove Creek Gap, NC w ❧ Named for Andy C. Bennett, who once lived in the Cataloochee Creek area of what is now the park. Formerly called Hannah Branch.

Andy McCully Branch Calderwood, TN/NC ne **Andy McCully Ridge** Calderwood, TN/NC e-ne ❧ Named for a farmer who cultivated a large part of this area before park establishment. His farm included parts of the ridge.

Anthony Branch #1 Noland Creek, NC w **Anthony Branch #2** Silers Bald, NC/TN w **Anthony Cemetery** Noland Creek, NC w **Anthony Ridge** Cades Cove, TN/NC ne-e **Anthony Right Prong** Cades Cove, TN/NC e ***n.l.*** ❧ Named for an Anthony family that settled on the northeast end of Cades Cove in the 1830s. They migrated to Hazel Creek and other areas in the late 1800s.

Anthony Creek Cades Cove, TN/NC ne ❧ Named for the John Anthony family, pioneers who settled near the Left and Right Prongs of this creek in the 1830s.

Appalachian Mountains ❧ Named for the Apalachees, a Native American tribe that Hernando de Soto and his Spanish explorers found living along the Gulf of Mexico, in the panhandle of Florida, circa 1540.

Arbutus Branch Cades Cove, TN/NC nw **Arbutus Ridge** Cades Cove, TN/NC nw ❥ Named for the wildflower, trailing arbutus (*Epigaea repens*), which is abundant in this area. Trailing arbutus is one of the first wildflowers to bloom in the Great Smoky Mountains in the spring.

Arch Rock Mt. Le Conte, TN/NC s ❥ A natural stone arch formed by freeze-thaw erosion in dense black slate. Alum Cave Trail passes through arch rock.

Asbury Trail Cove Creek Gap, NC s-m-w ❥ Named for Bishop Francis Asbury, father of American Methodism, and the first of the circuit riding preachers to penetrate the wilds of the Great Smoky Mountains. He is known to have traveled through the Smokies at least 60 times during the 1780s and 1790s. Formerly part of the longer Cataloochee Trail, it is now maintained by area scout troops.

Asgini Branch Cades Cove, TN/NC e **Asgini Ridge** Cades Cove, TN/NC e-se ❥ This is the Cherokee term for devil. See Devil Branch.

Ash Camp Branch Silers Bald, NC/TN n-nw ❥ 1. The name probably refers to forest fire damage along this stream that park records show occurred extensively in the 1920s, and to some degree before and after. See Fire Cherry Branch. 2. Name could also refer to the white ash (*Fraxinus americana*) or green ash (*F. Pennsylvanica*) both of which are found in the park. The camp part of the name could refer to an old lumber, hunting, or fishing camp once located along this stream.

Ash hopper

Ash Hopper Branch Gatlinburg, TN e ❥ Named for a V-shaped wooden structure (a large hopper) used for leaching ashes to recover their alkali salts for making lye soap and hominy. Such a hopper was once located on this stream. An example can be seen today at the Mountain Farm Museum at the Oconaluftee Visitor Center.

Ashley Branch Wear Cove, TN s ❧ Probably named for a W. Ashley Moore (1885–1941), daughter of Loon Grant Moore and his wife Elizabeth, who lived on nearby Loan (Loon) Branch. Formerly called Cane Branch for river cane growing along its banks.

Augerhole Gap Fontana Dam, NC ne ❧ This name probably relates to early copper mining in this area, since it is on land formerly owned by the North Carolina Exploration Company. The Tennessee Valley Authority acquired this part of their land holdings for development of Fontana Dam and Reservoir and later transferred it to the National Park Service. Auger holes were bored into rock, packed with explosives, and detonated to blast loose ore.

Bald Branch Clingmans Dome, NC/TN sw ❧ So named because this stream drains Andrews Bald.

Bald Range Cades Cove, TN/NC sw *n.l.* ❧ Name refers to a number of previously larger meadows or treeless areas, called balds, along a 24-mile section of the state line ridge, in the western end of the park. The main balds (from east to west) are Silers Bald, Spence Field, Little Bald, Russell Field, Gregory Bald, and Parson Bald.

Gregory Bald

Ballhoot Scar Overlook Smokemont, NC se ❧ Ballhooting is a logger's term for moving logs by sliding or rolling them down slope. The scars from this former timbering activity are still visible in this area today, and can be seen clearly from this overlook.

Balsam (Balsam Corner,* Balsam Mountain, Balsam Point, etc.)** ❧ All names are in reference to the balsam fir (*Abies balsamea*), a fragrant evergreen tree found in the northern Appalachians. It is a close relative of the Fraser fir (*Abies fraseri*) which grows at high elevations in the southern Appalachians, including in the park. In the past, many people referred to Fraser firs as "balsams." *The term "corner" often refers to a survey point where a property line turns left or right, at some angle, before continuing on. Balsam Corner was marked by a fir tree, on a rock, at the junction of Mount Sterling Ridge and Balsam Ridge, as noted in a land survey of 1898. Formerly called the Big Swag. **Formerly called Master Knob. Arnold H. Guyot (see Mount Guyot) called this peak Neighbor Knob, but the name never was widely accepted.

Bark Camp Run Kinzel Springs, TN sw ❧ Probably named for early tanbark harvesting in this area. Eastern hemlocks, American chestnuts, and oaks were cut down and their bark stripped and sold to tanneries. Tannin was extracted from the bark and used to cure leather. The term camp suggests that the tan bark harvesters may have lived somewhere along the stream while they were working here. A "run" is a small stream, often fairly straight and swift. See also Spud Town Branch.

Barnes Branch #1* Hartford, TN/NC se **Barnes Branch #2** Luftee Knob, NC/TN ne ❧ Named for the Barnes families that settled in these areas and gave their names to Barnes Valley, Barnes Valley School, and so forth. *Tom Barnes, for whom this stream was named, was a well known bear hunter.

Bas Shaw Cemetery Calderwood, TN/NC s ***n.s.*** ❧ Named for the grave of a Union soldier by the name of Bas Shaw who was killed by North Carolina raiders and buried here near Deals Gap.

Basin Spring Mt. Le Conte, TN/NC s ***n.s.*** ❧ Believed to be named for this spring that emerges from a large basin, beneath the summit of Mount Le Conte. Le Conte Lodge is situated in this basin.

Baskins Creek Mt. Le Conte, TN/NC w **Baskins Creek Falls** Mt. Le Conte, TN/NC w ***n.s.*** ❧ 1. According to legend, a bear hunter named Bear Skin Joe had a cabin on this stream. The stream was originally called Bear Skin Joe's Creek, but as time went on the bear skin was shortened and the Joe was dropped, hence Baskins Creek. 2. Said to be a favorite place in the early days to stretch bear pelts for drying, hence bearskins or B'a'skins, and now Baskins.

Batsaw Branch Smokemont, NC ne ❧ 1. Name may be a corruption of Bradshaw, for a family that settled in the Smokies in the 1850s or 1860s. 2. Name may be a variation of Bas Shaw (See Bas Shaw Cemetery). 3. Name may also somehow relate to early logging operations in the area. Formerly called Balsam Branch.

Battle Branch Silers Bald, NC/TN n **Battle Hollow** Silers Bald, NC/TN n ❧ 1. Battle Branch and Battle Hollow are located near Hostility Branch. All names refer to the fact that the country was so rough you had to battle your way through it. War Branch is also located just downstream. 2. They were named for a battle board, a type of scrub board used by women to wash laundry in a stream.

Baxter Creek Cove Creek Gap, NC nw ❧ Named for Steven Baxter, a long-time resident of this area. He was involved in the timber industry prior to park establishment.

Beard Cane Creek, Beard Cane Gap, Beard Cane Mountain Kinzel Springs, TN sw ❧ Probably named for a Beard (or Baird) family that settled along this stream where river cane was abundant. River cane (or switch cane) (*Arundinaria tecta*) is a native bamboo plant. Much of this cane disappeared from what is now the park in years past. It was overgrazed as winter forage, especially by hogs that destroyed its root systems.

Bear deadfall trap

Bearpen (as in Bearpen Branch, Bearpen Hollow, Bearpen Ridge, etc.) ❧ Named for the presence of heavy deadfall traps, called bear pens.

Bearwallow Bald Silers Bald, NC/TN sw **Bear Wallow Branch #1** Gatlinburg, TN s **Bear Wallow Branch #2** Mt. Guyot, TN/NC s **Bearwallow Ridge** Silers Bald, NC/TN w-sw ❥ Named for the presence of bearwallows, or natural bear bath tubs, of soft, mossy, moisture-laden soil in shallow rock depressions. Bears bathe or wallow in them.

Black bear

Beaugard Ridge Bryson City, NC n ❥ Name is probably a variation of Bogart (Beaugard is the German spelling of the name), for a family of early settlers in this area.

Beck Cemetery Smokemont, NC m **Becks Bald** Smokemont, NC ne-n **Becks Branch** Smokemont, NC m-e ❥ Named for a Beck family (most likely John Beck's family), who settled in the Oconaluftee Valley around 1804.

Bee Bait Ridge Calderwood, TN/NC w-m-n-nw ***n.l.*** ❥ Named for a substance called bee bait, once used to attract bees so they could be followed back to their natural tree hives, captured, and transplanted into domestic hives (or bee gums). The substance was composed of honey, maple syrup, or some other sweetener mixed with water.

Beech (Beech Creek, Beech Flats, etc.) ❥ Named for the American beech tree (*Fagus grandifolia*).

Beech Gap Luftee Knob, NC/TN s ❥ Beech gaps are groves of American beech trees found along ridge tops where they seem to withstand the effects of heavy wind, rain, ice, snow, and lightning strikes better than many other hardwood species.

Bee Gum Branch #1 Noland Creek, NC n-ne **Bee Gum Branch #2*** Thunderhead Mt., NC/TN se ❥ Bee gums are home-made bee hives crafted from the hollow logs of blackgum trees. Blackgums (*Nyssa sylvatica*) are susceptible to a disease called heart rot, which makes them hollow. Unlike some woods, they also tend not to split as they dry out or cure. To construct bee hives (or gums), one need only attach boards to the bottom and top of a short section of hollow blackgum log. *Also has been called Raven Den Branch.

Bell Branch Calderwood, TN/NC n-nw **Bell Cove Branch** Calderwood, TN/NC e ❧ Probably named for the presence of silverbell trees (*Halesia carolina*) also known as bellwood or peawood.

Bee gums

Bennett Branch Cove Creek Gap, NC s ❧ Named for a Bennett family that settled in the Cataloochee Valley in the 1830s and Little Cataloochee Valley in the late 1850s.

Ben Parton Overlook Silers Bald, NC/TN nw ❧ Named for a former Little River Lumber Company employee. He built a platform at this locale from which to watch for trespassers and wildfires within the lumber company domain.

Bent Arm Silers Bald, NC/TN n-nw ❧ Thought to describe the crooked east end of Miry Ridge. See also Dripping Spring Mountain.

Bettis Branch Cove Creek Gap, NC nw ❧ Probably named for a John Bettis family that settled in this area in 1862.

Bible Creek Calderwood, TN/NC s-se ❧ This name was probably coined because the stream originates on Parson Bald. There is also a New Testament Branch on Parson Bald, but it is not labeled on current maps.

Big Abrams Gap Cades Cove, TN/NC e ❧ See Abrams Creek.

Big Bald Branch Dellwood, NC w ❧ Probably named for Hemphill Bald, a large treeless area situated on the Cataloochee Divide and extending from Double Gap southwest to Pine Tree Gap.

Big Butt Luftee Knob, NC/TN m-e ❧ A butt in local vernacular usually refers to an abrupt, broken off end of a ridge or mountain. It can also refer to a promontory or headland; a hillock or mound; a short broad projection from the lower part of a mountain.

Big Cataloochee Mountain Luftee Knob, NC/TN m-e-s-se ❧ Formerly called Big Cataloochee, Big Cataloochee Knob, Big Cataluche, Big Catalychee, Cataloochee Mountain, and Luftee Knob. At an elevation of 6,155 feet above sea level, this is the tenth highest free-standing peak in the park. See also Cataloochee.

Big Chestnut Bald Thunderhead Mt., NC/TN e ❧ This bald probably had a large number of American chestnut trees on or around it until a blight destroyed this species in the park (in the 1920s) and later throughout the U.S. The trees could also have been intentionally killed in the early days to create an artificial bald or pasture for grazing. The general area of Big Chestnut Bald and Derrick Knob were once called Hall Cabin, for a prominent home located in the area. See also Hall Cabin.

Grill Ridge Cades Cove, TN/NC se-e ❧ Origin unknown. Formerly called Big Drill Ridge, and for this reason, the name may be related to early mining or prospecting operations in this area.

Big Head Branch Luftee Knob w ❧ Name may relate to a knob to the southwest that looks something like a large head.

Big Hollow #1 Gatlinburg, TN s **Big Hollow #2** Thunderhead Mt., NC/TN n ❧ A hollow, or "holler" in the vernacular of mountain folk, is a small valley between mountains.

Big Horseshoe Cades Cove, TN/NC nw *n.l.* ❧ Named for the mile-and-one-quarter-long, horseshoe-shaped bend on Abrams Creek that winds around the southwest end of Arbutus Ridge. Anglers frequently become lost in this area because of the confusing course of the stream.

Big Medicine Branch Gatlinburg, TN s-se **Big Medicine Gap** Thunderhead Mt., NC/TN ne ❧ Name may refer to the term medicine as it was used by Native Americans to describe objects, spells, or rites that were believed to have supernatural powers.

Big Slick Ridge Clingmans Dome, NC/TN w ❧ Probably named for the presence of laurel slicks on this ridge. Laurel slicks are thick, tangled, and almost impenetrable vegetation; mostly mountain laurel, rhododendron, dog-hobble, or similar dense, evergreen, shrubby growth. When seen from a distance, they appear slick or smooth in comparison to surrounding forests.

Big Spring Cove Thunderhead Mt., NC/TN nw ❧ Named for a small cove containing several sink holes and a large spring. Geologically, it is a miniature version of nearby Whiteoak Sinks. Formerly called Big Spring Meadow, Laurel Creek Sinks, Sinks Meadow, and Spruce Flats (for the presence of hemlocks, which mountain folk often call spruce).

Big Spruce Ridge Bunches Bald, NC e ❧ Named for the presence of eastern hemlock trees (*Tsuga canadensis*) that mountain folk often refer to as spruce or spruce pine. True spruce (red) are found at higher elevations (generally above 4,000 feet).

Big Swag Cades Cove, TN/NC se ❧ A swag is a gap or depression along a ridge or mountain top, a sag.

Bill Deadening Branch Gatlinburg, TN m ❧ Named for a Bill, surname unknown, who deadened (girdled and killed) the trees along this stream to prepare new ground for cultivation.

Birchfield Branch Fontana Dam, NC n-ne ❧ Named for a Birchfield family that settled in the Hazel Creek area in the 1880s or 1890s.

Black Camp Branch, Black Camp Gap Bunches Bald, NC s ❧ So named because a forest fire once partially burned a rustic structure in this camp that was often used by hunters as well as farmers ranging cattle in this area. Thereafter, campers often got black soot on themselves when they stayed in the partially charred structure.

Black Fox Branch Mt. Le Conte, TN/NC nw ❧ Of the two species of foxes in the park, the red and the gray, the red is often so dark it appears black. This is thought to be the origin of this name.

Black Gum Branch Calderwood, TN/NC s-se **Black Gum Gap** Calderwood, TN/NC se ❧ Named for the blackgum trees (*Nyssa sylvatica*) common in this area.

Blanket Mountain fire tower

Blanket Creek Gatlinburg, TN sw ❧ 1. Named for Blanket Mountain (see next listing). 2. So named because people used to stretch a blanket overhead for shelter as they camped along this stream.

Blanket Mountain Gatlinburg, TN sw ❧ 1. Name resulted from an 1802 boundary survey when Return Jonathan Meigs (see Meigs Mountain) suspended a brightly colored blanket from the top of a tall tree on this mountain as a site point for a surveyor on another nearby peak. 2. Name resulted from Indians using this peak to send smoke signals (using a smoky fire and blanket).

Blazed Balsam Clingmans Dome, NC/TN w ***n.l.*** ❧ Named for a survey tree, a Fraser (often called balsam) fir, marked on the state line during the Davenport Survey of 1821.

Blazed Pine Ridge Mt. Le Conte, TN/NC ne ❧ Probably named for a blazed pine tree once used as a survey point on this ridge.

Blight Branch Wear Cove, TN sw *n.s.* ❧ Could have been named for the non-native fungal blight that killed the American chestnut trees in the park. See also Chestnut Branch.

Blockade (Branch) Creek Bryson City, NC n *n.s.* ❧ An old Smoky Mountain term, probably derived from the Irish practice of defying, or running, the British blockade in regard to uncontrolled or untaxed liquor. The terms blockade and moonshine were used interchangeably.

Blockhouse Mountain Thunderhead Mt., NC/TN w-m **Blockhouse Ridge** Thunderhead Mt., NC/TN m-w-s ❧ So named because illegal moonshine liquor was once made in these areas. They were wild, almost impenetrable areas that Federal Revenue Agents had trouble getting into and out of. The block part of the name is probably rooted in the word blockade (see Blockade Creek). There may also have been a structure here at one time that would account for the "house" part of the name.

Bloody Branch Wear Cove, TN se ❧ So named because a number of domestic hogs were slaughtered along this stream. The pigs had been left to range freely through the mountains, as was the practice in the early years, and had become too wild to be herded back to their owner's farm.

Blount County, Tennessee ❧ Named for William Blount, governor of the Territory South of the River Ohio, established in 1795. The territorial capital was at Knoxville, Tennessee. William was the leader of the so-called "Blount Conspiracy," for which he was expelled by the Senate in 1797 and immediately impeached by the House. In 1799 the Senate failed to convict him of charges that he illegally conspired with England to take control of Spanish-held Florida and Louisiana. His failures on the national scene did not hamper his return to state politics.

Blowdown Thunderhead Mt., NC/TN n ❧ Named for an area where a wide swath of tuliptrees and other trees were blown down by a storm in 1875. One early reference calls the storm a hurricane. Dying hurricanes from the Atlantic Ocean and Gulf of Mexico sometimes bring surprisingly high winds and heavy rains to the Great Smoky Mountains, especially at the higher elevations. This was the site of an early Little River Lumber Company logging camp. See also Hurricane Branch.

Blowhole Cave Wear Cove, TN sw ***n.l.*** ❧ So named because air emanates from a narrow entrance to this cave. The caves of this cove maintain a constant temperature of 56 degrees F., which is the average mean temperature for the region. Air from the blowhole feels refreshingly cool in summer and pleasantly warm and damp on cold winter days. (Note: a permit is required to enter all park caves.)

Bluff Branch Tuskeegee, NC e ❧ Named for the once prominent bluffs along the Little Tennessee River, now submerged beneath the waters of Fontana Lake.

Board Camp Creek, Board Camp Gap Silers Bald, NC/TN se ❧ Named for a cabin used by hunters at this gap. The structure was built of rough-sawn boards.

Bogle Branch Silers Bald, NC/TN w ***n.l.*** ❧ A bogle is a sawmill truck, a hobgoblin, or a bogy (bogeyman). Which one applies to this place name is unknown. The name might also refer to a Bogle family that once lived in the area.

Bone Valley Thunderhead Mt., NC/TN s **Bone Valley Creek** Thunderhead Mt., NC/TN s-m ❧ Prior to park establishment, farmers in this area drove their cattle to higher pastures each spring. In 1888, a farmer drove his cattle to this valley too early in the spring. A freak blizzard trapped them, and without shelter they froze to death. The area's name is derived from the presence of the bleached bones of these cattle that lay in this valley for many years.

Boogerman Trail Dellwood, NC n-nw *n.l.* ❧ Named for Robert Palmer, a local resident, whose nickname was Boogerman. As a child, Robert was very bashful. When asked in school one day what he wanted to be when he grew up, he put his head down on his desk and laughed, "The Boogerman." The name stuck. As he grew older, he sported a bushy beard that gave him an intimidating and frightening appearance. It is said that he liked to take advantage of this look to scare children. He was very reclusive in his later years and refused to sell his land or timber rights to the lumber companies. Hence, the virgin forest through which his namesake trail passes, was preserved as a legacy to the man. His father was Turkey George Palmer, another well known and colorful Smoky Mountain resident.

Boomer Branch Silers Bald, NC/TN w ❧ Named for the red squirrel (*Tamiasciurus hudsonicus*) alias "boomer," known for its noisy chatter and ratchet-like calls.

Red squirrel

Boring Ridge Cades Cove, TN/NC nw-w **Boring Cemetery*** Calderwood, TN/NC n ❧ Named for the Boring family that farmed this area prior to park establishment. *May have been named specifically for William Boring, a Baptist minister, and his wife and three children who died here during a late 1800s typhoid epidemic.

Bote Mountain Thunderhead Mt., NC/TN nw ❧ While constructing the Anderson Turnpike that was to run from Tuckaleechee Cove across the Smokies to the Tuckaseegee settlements in North Carolina, an engineer had to decide which of two ridge top routes to follow. Several Cherokees, asked which route they would choose, voted unanimously for the one along this mountain by pointing to it and saying "bote," (there is no "v" sound in the Cherokee language). The other ridge, the loser, was thereafter referred to as Defeat Ridge. A variation of this story says that it was German immigrants, not Indians, who said "bote."

Boulevard Prong Mt. Le Conte, TN/NC s-se-e **Boulevard, The** Mt. Le Conte, TN/NC s-se **Boulevard Trail** Mt. Le Conte, TN/NC s-se *n.l.* ❧ Before a path was cleared along the high ridge to connect Mount Le Conte with the Appalachian Trail, a hiker, inching his way through the torturous vines and shrubs, was heard referring to the thoroughfare as, "That damned boulevard." The prong (stream) and trail were named for the ridge.

Logging train

Boxcar Curve Wear Cove, TN m ***n.l.*** ➧ When the Little River Road was the bed of the Little River Railroad, a caboose (or possibly a boxcar used as a caboose) came loose from a logging train and ran all the way back down the track to this curve, where it derailed into the river.

Bradley Fork Smokemont, NC n-m **Bradley Fork Valley** Smokemont, NC m ➧ Named for the Isaac, Andrew Jackson or Jack Bradley family. The Bradleys migrated from Rutherford County, North Carolina, to settle on the Oconaluftee River and this tributary that bears their name.

Brakeshoe Spring Luftee Knob, NC/TN ne ➧ So named because a logging train engineer once placed a locomotive brakeshoe into a hole in a rock at this location creating a curved flow drinking fountain. The brakeshoe disappeared in the mid 1970s, but the name remains.

Bratcher Gap Cove Creek Gap, NC sw ➧ Named for J. Bratcher Bradshaw who acquired land in Haywood County, North Carolina in 1797.

Breakfast Branch Wear Cove, TN e-se ➧ According to one source, when John Huskey and his son took apples to market in Knoxville, Tennessee, they would leave their home in the Meigs community before dawn and eat breakfast beside this stream at daybreak.

Breakneck Ridge Luftee Knob, NC/TN sw ❧ Probably named for the ruggedness of the terrain on this ridge, where travelers could easily break their necks if they were to fall.

Brier Lick Branch Cades Cove, TN/NC s-sw **Brier Lick Gap, Brier Lick Knob** Cades Cove, TN/NC s ❧ Named for a brierlick, a patch of blackberries, greenbrier, or other such thorny bushes.

Brushy Mountain Mt. Le Conte, TN/NC m ❧ Much of Brushy Mountain is covered by a heath bald—a dense thicket of mountain laurel, rhododendron, sand myrtle, and other shrubs or "brush."

Bryson Branch Clingmans Dome, NC/TN s-se ***n.s.*** ❧ 1. Named for the Col. Thaddeus Dillary Bryson family, early residents of this area, and founders of Bryson City, North Carolina. 2. Named for an Elliott Bryson who lived here in the mid 1800s. This area was a favorite retreat for Horace Kephart (see Mount Kephart) and others, prior to park establishment.

Buckeye Cove Silers Bald, NC/TN nw **Buckeye Creek** Jones Cove, TN se **Buckeye Gap*** Silers Bald, NC/TN w **etc.** ❧ Named for the yellow buckeye (*Aesculus octandra*), a common tree in the park. *This is believed to have been the Frog Place (Walasiyi) of Cherokee mythology, the home of a giant, mystical, green frog. Cherokee legend has it that once during a battle, they captured a Shawano (magician). As they prepared to torture him to death, he pleaded with them, promising that if they would release him, he would use his strong medicine to capture the great serpent Uktena for them. This creature had a magnificent, mystical, blazing star set in its forehead and he who possessed it would have great power. During his search for the great Uktena, the magician came upon the Walasiyi or "Frog Place," believed to be Buckeye Gap. (Other sources say the location was Mt. Le Conte.) When the other Indians came to look upon the gap, they saw a monster frog squatting there and were frightened away. The magician laughed at their fear of a frog, albeit a giant one, and continued his search for Uktena.

Bull Cave Kinzel Springs, TN s ❧ This name refers to an incident where a bull fell down into a deep sinkhole near the entrance of this cave. The bull was part of a cattle drive over the mountains along the Rich Mountain Road. (Note: a permit is required to enter all park caves.)

Bullhead Mt. Le Conte, TN/NC sw **Bullhead Branch** Gatlinburg, TN e-se ❧ 1. Bullhead is named for its resemblance to a male buffalo's head. 2. Named for Uskwalena, one of the old Cherokee chiefs whose name translates to bull head or Big head. 3. Named for John "Bullhead" Whaley, an early resident of this area.

Bumgardner Branch, Bumgardner Ridge Clingmans Dome, NC/TN s ❧ Named for Cindy Bumgardner who owned property in this area.

Bunches Creek Bunches Bald, NC s-m ❧ 1. Thought to be named for a lumberman by the name of Bunche who operated in this area prior to park establishment. Formerly called Bunch Creek. 2. May also be named for the presence of bunch-flowers (*Melanthium latifolium*) along this stream.

Bunker Hill Calderwood, TN/NC s **Bunker Hill Branch** Calderwood, TN/NC sw-s **Bunker Hill Lead** Calderwood, TN/NC se-s ❧ This prominent peak is thought to have been given this name for no particular reason except that it needed a name and someone suggested Bunker Hill, a patriotic one. It was not uncommon in the early days to name places after other famous places or people.

Bunting Branch Cades Cove, TN/NC n-m ❧ Probably named for the bird, the Indigo Bunting (*Passerina cyanea*). It is a common summer inhabitant of the park at low and mid elevations.

Burr Branch Wear Cove, TN sw ❧ Probably named for chestnut burrs, the prickly, outer husks that enclose the nuts of this once prominent tree. See Chestnut Branch.

Butt Mountain Luftee Knob, NC/TN se ❧ See glossary for butt.

Cable Branch Fontana Dam, NC ne ❧ Named for the Samuel Cable family that settled here circa 1835.

View of Cades Cove

Cades Branch Cades Cove, TN/NC m-n **Cades Cove** Cades Cove, TN/NC nw-n-ne ❧ There are several possible origins for this name. 1. Named for a Cherokee chief Cade (or Kade) who once claimed land in the cove. 2. Name is a variation of Kates Cove, for Cherokee Chief Abrams' wife, known to the settlers as Kate. 3. Named for the Cades, a family of white settlers that once lived in the cove. 4. A variation of Cage Cove, so called because some people felt caged in by the mountains surrounding this cove. The most compelling argument seems to favor Chief Cade or Kade. An old Indian name for the cove was Tsiyahi, which translates to Otter's Place. See also Cheoah Lake.

Caldwell Fork*, Caldwell Fork Valley Bunches Bald, NC e ❧ Named for a Caldwell (Coldwell) family that settled in the Cataloochee Valley in the 1830s and the Little Cataloochee Valley in the late 1850s. *John Caldwell had a house and farm on this stream.

Calhoun Branch #1 Thunderhead Mt., NC/TN m **Calhoun Branch #2** Tuskeegee, NC m-n ➧ Named for one of the first families to settle in the Hazel Creek area. Joshua Calhoun was the first, arriving circa 1880. Granville Calhoun was called the Squire of Hazel Creek because he was a country gentleman, a prominent citizen, and a major land owner.

Camel Gap Luftee Knob, NC/TN n ➧ 1. Named for a Camel family that once lived at this gap. 2. Could be a corruption of the family name Campbell.

Cammerer Ridge Hartford, TN/NC s-se ➧ See Mount Cammerer.

Carlos Campbell

Campbell Overlook Gatlinburg, TN se ***n.l.*** ➧ Named for Carlos Campbell who, in the 1920s, served as manager of the Knoxville Chamber of Commerce. He was interested in establishing a national park in the Smokies, as an investment in the region. Unfortunately, he eventually had to leave his job when other members asserted that he was spending too much time promoting the park and not enough time on other matters. Fortunately, he lived long enough to see the Smokies become one of the most successful projects ever undertaken by the Chamber. He worked for a time with Jim Thompson's Photographic Studio in Knoxville and accompanied Thompson on photographic treks into the park. The classic Thompson photos, some published by *National Geographic* magazine, brought much attention to the Smokies and its unique natural and cultural heritage. Campbell was the author of an authoritative book on the park entitled, *Birth of a National Park.* According to Edward J. Meeman, first editor of the Knoxville *News-Sentinel*, "Carlos C. Campbell . . . became the best informed man on the Great Smoky Mountains, the most understanding, courageous and persistent friend the park project, and later the park itself, ever had." This site was formerly known as the Big Walnut Overlook.

Camp (Margaret) Townsend Wear Cove, TN s ➧ Named in honor of the wife of Colonel Wilson B. Townsend, owner of the Little

River Lumber Company, and the man for whom the town of Townsend was named. Formerly the site of the Margaret Townsend Girl Scout Camp, and now occupied by the Great Smoky Mountains Institute at Tremont, an environmental education center.

Camp Rock Backcountry Campsite Silers Bald, NC/TN n *n.s.* ❧ Formerly named for an overhanging rock ledge, one mile downstream of this present site. It once provided campers some protection against the elements. The campsite was eventually moved upstream by the National Park Service, but kept its original name.

Camp Ten Branch Cades Cove, TN/NC se ❧ Ten was probably the number of a lumber company camp located on this stream.

Canadian Top Cove Creek Gap, NC sw ❧ 1. Named for a John Canadian, also known as John the Canadian or John Ewart, a Canadian. He was an early Haywood County, North Carolina lumberjack. 2. Named for Bill and Nancy Ewart, who because they were from Canada, were also known as Bill and Nancy Canadian.

Canebreak Branch (Bryson City, NC w-nw) **Cane Creek #1** Blockhouse, TN se **Cane Creek #2** Wear Cove, TN m **Cane Gap** Blockhouse, TN se **Canepatch Ridge** Fontana Dam, NC n **and other cane-related place names** ❧ Named for the dense stands of switch cane, (*Arundinaria tecta*) a native bamboo plant, found in these areas. Much of this cane disappeared from what is now the park in years past. It was overgrazed as winter forage, especially by hogs that destroyed its root systems, and hence its ability to spread and reproduce.

Cannon Creek Mt. Le Conte, TN/NC m-e-s ❧ Probably named for a Sevier County, Tennessee, Cannon family that once lived on or near this stream.

Carr Branch Gatlinburg, TN m-e ❧ Named for a Carr (or Kear) family that once settled in the Forks of the River and the Sugarlands areas. Also see Kear Branch.

Cataloochee Balsam* Bunches Bald, NC m **Cataloochee Creek** Cove Creek Gap, NC sw-s-m **Cataloochee Divide** Bunches Bald, NC e **Cataloochee Valley** Cove Creek Gap, NC m-s-sw ***n.l.*** ❧ A corruption of the Cherokee term Gadalutsi that is variously translated as "fringe standing erect," "waves of mountains," "wave upon wave," "land of plenty," "in a row," and "standing in ranks." It is thought to be descriptive of trees standing in a row along narrow ridge crests. Also spelled Cataluche, Cattalooch, Cataloocha, Cattyloochy, and Catalooch. *Also see Balsam Mountain.

Waves of Smoky Mountains

Cataract Branch* Gatlinburg, TN m-e **Cataract Falls** Gatlinburg, TN e ***n.s.*** ❧ Cataract is a term meaning waterfall or cascading falls. *Formerly called Fall Branch.

Cat Stairs, Cat Stairs Branch Mt. Guyot, TN/NC nw ❧ This name refers to a very steep and precarious route up the northwest side of Greenbrier Pinnacle. It is said a cat could climb this route easier than a human.

Cave Ridge Cades Cove, TN/NC n ❧ So named because Gregory Cave is located on the lower flanks of this ridge.

Cerulean Knob Kinzel Springs, TN se ❧ 1. Cerulean means blue and the name may simply be descriptive of the blue sky seen from this high point. 2. May be named for the Cerulean Warbler (*Dendroica cerulea*) that is a shade of blue said to be the color of cobalt stannate. This bird is rare in the park.

Chambers Branch, Chambers Creek *n.l.*, Chambers Creek Gap Noland Creek, NC nw ❥ Named for some Chambers families on the North Carolina side of the park. John Chambers, for example, was an early settler in Swain County, North Carolina, and the James Chambers family was among the first settlers in adjacent Haywood County, circa 1780s.

Chapman Lead, Chapman Prong Mt. Guyot, TN/NC m-e ❥ Named in honor of Col. David Chapman (1876–1938), a Knoxville pharmacist who championed the acquisition and development of the park. He chaired the Tennessee Great Smoky Mountains National Park Commission and is called the father of the Great Smoky Mountains National Park.

Charlies Bunion

Charlies Bunion Mt. Guyot, TN/NC sw ❥ This name was wittingly given to a rocky promontory along the Sawteeth Range (and the Appalachian Trail) by Horace Kephart, a local writer (see Mount Kephart). The origin of this name has been variously interpreted by numerous writers, but the essence is as follows: On a trip to survey erosion damage resulting from an intense 1929 storm, Kephart described the craggy formation as having the "Knobby appearance of Charlie Conner's bunion." Charlie was a member of the survey party who had a foot problem that day, and was hobbling along. When interviewed later about the incident, Conners did not recall having a bunion. It was a colorful name that the U.S. Geological Survey couldn't resist. Formerly called Fodderstack.

Chasteen Creek Smokemont, NC m-n-ne **Chasteen Creek Cascade** Smokemont, NC n ***n.s.*** ❧ Named for Chasteen Reagan, a colorful mountain man, hunter, trapper, and early settler in this area.

Cheoah Lake Fontana Dam, NC w-nw-m ❧ Cheoah, Cheowa, Cheeowhee, Chewohe, and Chewe are all variations of Tsiyahi, a word that means Otter Place in the Cherokee language.

Cherokee Orchard Mt. Le Conte, TN/NC w ❧ Named for a commercial apple orchard and plant nursery once owned and operated by M. M. Whittle. It was established in the 1920s and named for the Cherokee Indian legacy of the area. With the coming of the park, the orchard, containing over 6,000 fruit trees, as well as other ornamental trees and shrubs, was abandoned. The word Cherokee, in their language, means cave people.

Cherry Orchard Mt. Guyot TN/NC n ***n.l.*** ❧ Named for the great number of very large black cherry trees (*Prunus serotina*) growing in this area.

Chestnut Branch* Hartford, TN/NC se **Chestnut Cove** Thunderhead Mt., NC/TN s ***n.s.*** **Chestnut Top** Wear Cove, TN sw **and other chestnut-related names** ❧ Named for the ill-fated American chestnut tree (*Castanea dentata*). Until its park-wide destruction by an imported Chinese fungal blight, from 1928 through 1940, it was a dominant tree in the eastern forest. *Also once known as Old Mother. See also Mount Cammerer.

Chickadee Branch Cades Cove, TN/NC w ❧ 1. Probably named for an attractive and active little bird called a chickadee (*Parus* sp.) 2. A chickadee is also a nickname (logging term) for a man who took care of the logging roads.

Chilhowee, Chilhowee Lake Tallassee, TN e ❧ Chilhowee is a Cherokee term that one source defines as "the valley of many deer" and another as "deer burning." Chilhowee was the site of a Cherokee Indian village. See also Abrams Creek.

Chiltoskie

Chiltoes Mountain Bunches Bald, NC n ❧ This name is probably a variation of Chiltoskie. See Chiltoskie Ridge.

Chiltoskie Ridge Bunches Bald, NC n-nw ❧ Named for an old Cherokee Indian that lived at the base of this ridge.

Chimney Tops Mt. Le Conte, TN/NC sw ❧ Named for two rock spires that from a distance look like chimneys. Nearly vertical shafts have eroded through the formation to create natural chimneys. The Cherokee name for this area was Duniskwa' lgun'yi meaning "Gap of the Forked Antler." Also called The Chimneys. The summit of the highest chimney is 4,755 feet.

The Chimney Tops

Chinquapin Knob, Chinquapin Ridge Gatlinburg, TN w ❧ Probably named for a tree now called the chinkapin oak (*Quercus muhlenbergii*) or the chinquapin (*Castanea pumila*), which does not occur in the park, or the American chestnut (*Castanea dentata*), which the chinquapin resembles. Boys and girls gathered and sold chinquapin (and chinquapin-like) nuts in the old days. They were often strung together with needle and thread to make necklaces that were a kid status symbol. As such, they were often used like Indian wampum as currency or as barter items.

Chokeberry Branch Silers Bald, NC/TN s-se ❧ Named for the red chokeberry (*Aronia* sp.), a shrub that grows along this stream and elsewhere in the park.

Clark Branch Tuskeegee, NC m **Clark Ridge** Thunderhead Mt., NC/TN e ***n.l.*** ❧ Named for a Clark family that settled along this stream. W. H. Clark still owned property here when the Tennessee Valley Authority (TVA) purchased land for development of the Fontana Dam and Reservoir in 1939.

Clingmans Creek, Clingmans Dome* Clingmans Dome, NC/TN w **Clingmans Dome Road**** Clingmans Dome, NC/TN w-nw-n ❧ Named for Brigadier General Thomas Lanier Clingman (1812–1897), soldier, mining expert, explorer, antebellum political leader, scientist, and all-around colorful character. He was the first man to accurately measure the height of his namesake peak in the 1850s. He was a staunch leader in the North Carolina Whig political party and, when the Civil War broke out, he joined the Confederacy. He first commanded the 25th Confederate Regiment as a colonel. Although wounded in action, he eventually rose to the rank of Brigadier General. Born in Huntsville, North Carolina, Clingman was part Cherokee on his mother's side; he lived in Asheville for 60 years. He was often described as a vain, conceited, but scholarly and brave man, who never married; he died impoverished and homeless.

Clingmans Dome observation tower

After the war, he was prohibited from returning to politics by the amnesty provisions, so he turned his interest to scientific investigations and the promotion and exploitation of the highlands of North Carolina. He had a long running debate with Dr. Elisha Mitchell of the University of North Carolina as to who first measured the highest peak in the East (now called Mt. Mitchell). Mitchell won the debate, but he died in 1857 while on an expedition to re-measure the mountain.

*The Cherokee called this mountain Kuwahi, "the Mulberry Place," where the mystical White Bear made his home. Formerly known as Smoky Dome and later Mount Buckley, at an elevation of 6,643 feet above sea level, it is the highest peak in

View from Clingmans Dome observation tower

the park and the highest elevation in the state of Tennessee. Seven states are said to be visible from the observation tower atop Clingmans Dome on a clear day. The mountain was named by geographer Arnold Guyot. (See also Mount Guyot and Kuwahi Branch.)

**Also called Skyland Drive, Skyland Highway, and Over-the-Mountain Highway, it is the highest paved road in eastern America, reaching a maximum elevation of about 6,300 feet.

Coalen Ground Branch, Coalen Ground Ridge Cades Cove, TN/NC w ❧ Named for an area where charcoal was produced in earthen pits called coalen(ing) grounds. The charcoal was used in forges to make iron from ore or for wroughting or shaping iron using hammers and other tools.

Cobb Butt,* Cobb Ridge Cades Cove, TN/NC m-e ❧ Named for a Cobb family, early residents of the Cades Cove area. *See butt in glossary.

Coburn Knob Clingmans Dome, NC/TN sw ❧ Named for Jack E. Coburn, of Bryson City, who was active in the movement to develop a national park in the Smokies.

Cocke County, Tennessee ➧ Named for William Cocke, Tennessee Senator and leader in establishment of the State of Franklin, which later became the state of Tennessee. The county seat is Newport.

Sawmill

Coffee Pot Creek Thunderhead Mt., NC/TN m-n *n.s.* ➧ Named for a coffee pot mill—a small, independent sawmill. See also Peckerwood Ridge.

Coggins Branch Cove Creek Gap, NC sw-w ➧ Named for former resident David Coggins, who is buried in Little Cataloochee Baptist Church Cemetery, within what is now the national park.

Coldspring Branch Fontana Dam, NC n-ne **Cold Spring Gap** Noland Creek, NC nw **Cold Spring Knob** Silers Bald, NC/TN w **Cold Water Knob** Thunderhead Mt., NC/TN nw-w **and other similar names** ➧ No spring is probably any colder or warmer than any other at the same elevation, but the higher the spring in elevation, the colder its water. Spring water and cave air maintain the approximate mean annual temperature of the area in which they are located.

Cole Creek #1 Jones Cove, TN se **Cole Creek #2** Mt. Le Conte, TN/NC sw ➧ Probably named for a Cole family that settled in the Forney Creek area in the early 1800s and moved out into other areas, including Forks of the River and Sugarlands.

Collins Creek Smokemont, NC w **Collins Gap** Clingmans Dome, NC/TN w ➧ See Mount Collins.

Conrad Branch Cove Creek Gap, NC sw-s ➧ Conrad was also spelled Koonrad and Conard. Conrad Branch was named for two Conrad families that lived in the Smokies in pre-park days. They were said to be reclusive families.

Cooks Creek Luftee Knob, NC/TN e-se **Cooks Knob** Cove Creek Gap, NC sw ➧ Named for Daniel J. Cook, an early settler who lived on land

NO POSTAGE
NECESSARY
IF MAILED
IN THE
UNITED STATES

BUSINESS REPLY MAIL

FIRST-CLASS MAIL PERMIT NO. 1158 BOULDER, CO

POSTAGE WILL BE PAID BY ADDRESSEE

PO BOX 51683
BOULDER CO 80323-1683

grant track #231a. He grazed cattle on this knob and trapped along Cooks Creek.

Coontown Branch Thunderhead Mt., NC/TN sw-w *n.s.* ❧ Probably named for the presence of raccoons along this stream.

Cooper Branch Cades Cove, TN/NC ne-n ❧ A Cooper family (or families) settled along this stream in the 1850s.

Cooper Road* Blockhouse, TN se **Cooper Road Trail** Cades Cove, TN/NC nw ❧ An early road connecting Cades Cove with Maryville and Knoxville. Completed in 1840, it was named for Joe Cooper, the man who supervised its construction. It was initially an Indian trail. *Formerly called Cane Creek Road.

Coot Cove Tuskeegee, NC e ❧ 1. Name may relate to a Smoky Mountain phrase, "to cooter around," meaning to wander aimlessly. 2. Possibly named for a foolish, eccentric, or senile person. 3. Probably not directly named for the American Coot (*Fulica americana*), a water bird that is rare in the park.

Cope Branch Thunderhead Mt., NC/TN s ❧ Named for a Cope family that settled in the Hazel Creek area in the late 1800s.

Copeland Creek Mt. Le Conte, TN/NC ne **Copeland Divide** Mt. Guyot, TN/NC nw ❧ Probably named for a Sevier County, Tennessee, Copeland family.

Copperhead Branch Mt. Guyot, TN/NC ne ❧ Named for one of the two species of venomous snakes in the park, the copperhead (*Agkistrodon contortrix*). See also Pilot Knob.

Cork Branch Cades Cove, TN/NC e-ne ❧ Boots with steel spikes imbedded in the soles were prized by loggers. They were almost a necessity for men whose lives often depended upon surefootedness on wet, slippery, debarked logs. Such boots were called calks, but the loggers pronounced the name corks.

Correll Branch Cove Creek Gap, NC w ❧ Named for J. Clark Correll who owned land and lived in this area. He was the general contractor on the Cataloochee Road project, constructed from Kerr Place on Cataloochee Creek to Mount Sterling Gap in the 1850s.

Cosby Creek Hartford, TN/NC sw-s **Cosby Knob** Luftee Knob, NC/TN n ❧ 1. Named in honor of Dr. James Cosby, one of the first physicians in Cocke County, Tennessee. 2. Named for an early trapper, John Cosby, who hunted on the west side of the Pigeon River along with John English for whom nearby English Mountain is named.

Couches Creek Smokemont, NC m-s-w ❧ Named for a settler who operated a gunpowder mill at the confluence of this stream and the Oconaluftee River beginning in 1834.

Cove Mountain Gatlinburg, TN w ❧ Probably named for Wear Cove, that lies to the northwest of this mountain and the park boundary.

Cowpen Top Cove Creek Gap, NC m ❧ In pre-park days, cattle were grazed along the tops of many ridges during the warmer months. In the fall, they were herded into fenced areas (or pens) prior to being driven back down to lower elevation winter pastures, to slaughter, or to market. See also Lawson Gant Lot.

Crestmont lumber mill and town

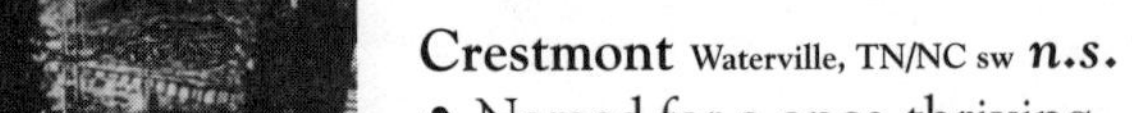

Crestmont Waterville, TN/NC sw *n.s.* ❧ Named for a once-thriving logging community, established in 1903 and probably operated by the Crestmont Lumber Company. The town was abandoned with the creation of the park. The name means mountain top.

Crib Gap Cades Cove, TN/NC ne ❧ Probably named for a corn crib once located at this site.

Cantilever corn crib

Crooked Arm, Crooked Arm Branch, Crooked Arm Falls Cades Cove, TN/NC ne ❧ Many of the older mountain people use the term arm to refer to a ridge or a spur of a ridge or mountain. This particular spur is crooked and some say in the shape of an elbow.

Cryin' Creek Hartford, TN/NC sw ❧ 1. Named for an incident that occurred along this stream in the early days. While hunting here, a man accidentally shot and killed his brother. He was so filled with grief over the incident that locals named the stream Cryin' Creek. 2. The former name of this stream, Crion Creek, may also relate (phonetically) to its name.

Cucumber Cove *n.l.*, Cucumber Gap Gatlinburg, TN s ❧ 1. Probably named for magnolia trees (*Magnolia* sp.) which have fruits that resemble cucumbers. 2. A wildflower called Indian cucumber also grows around Cucumber Gap.

Curry Gap Wear Cove, TN se **Curry He Mountain** Wear Cove, TN e-se **Curry Prong, Curry She Mountain** Wear Cove, TN se ❧ The names Curry He Mountain and Curry She Mountain resulted from a misunderstanding. A Cherokee man, referring to a plant used in spring salads (called gura), pointed to a peak and said "gura-hi," meaning that gura is found there. A local white man thought the Indian said curry he. Accordingly, a local woman, not to be slighted, named a nearby peak Curry She Mountain.

D

Dashoga Ridge Luftee Knob, NC/TN w-sw ❧ Dashoga is the Cherokee term for rhododendron (*rhododendron* sp.), a shrub that grows in abundance along this stream.

Davenport Gap Waterville, TN/NC sw ❧ Named for William Davenport, a native of North Carolina, and leader of a party that surveyed the state line through the Smokies in 1821.

Davidson Branch, Davidson Gap Cove Creek Gap, NC sw ❥ Named for a William Mitchell Davidson family of Jonathan Creek which herded cattle and hunted in this area. Their relatives were some of the first settlers in Haywood County, North Carolina, circa 1780s.

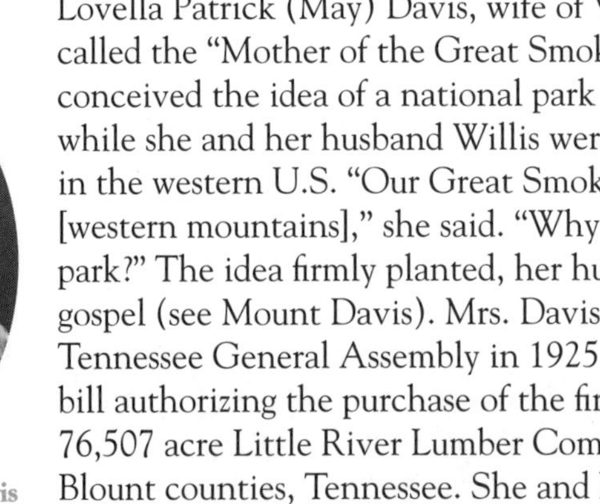

Davis Ridge Thunderhead Mt., NC/TN ne-e ❥ Named in honor of Ann Lovella Patrick (May) Davis, wife of Willis P. Davis, and often called the "Mother of the Great Smoky Mountains." She conceived the idea of a national park in the Smokies in 1923 while she and her husband Willis were visiting some of the parks in the western U.S. "Our Great Smokies are as beautiful as these [western mountains]," she said. "Why can't we have a national park?" The idea firmly planted, her husband began spreading the gospel (see Mount Davis). Mrs. Davis was elected to the Tennessee General Assembly in 1925 where she introduced a bill authorizing the purchase of the first large parcel of land, the 76,507 acre Little River Lumber Company track in Sevier and Blount counties, Tennessee. She and her husband loved the Smokies and often made mule back trips into the area. Formerly called Brier Ridge and Greenbrier Ridge.

Ann Davis

Deadrick Ridge Calderwood, TN/NC m ❥ Named for two brothers who settled on Panther Creek (#1) around the time of the Civil War. The family name was Deaderick, but in time the middle "e" was omitted from the ridge name.

Deals Branch Tapoco, NC/TN ne **Deals Gap** Tapoco, NC/TN n ❥ Named for a man called Deal who lived in the vicinity of this gap before the coming of Parsons Turnpike or Highways 129 and 72.

DeArmond Bald* Thunderhead Mt., NC/TN w-sw **DeArmond Ridge** Thunderhead Mt., NC/TN w ❥ Named for a DeArmond family that settled in Blount County, Tennessee. *Formerly called Little Fork Bald.

Deeplow Gap Clingmans Dome, NC/TN se ❥ This name is a combination of this gap's two former names, Deep Gap and Low Gap.

Deerhobble Branch, Deerhobble Ridge Thunderhead Mt., NC/TN m ❧ Probably so named because the vegetation on this ridge or along this stream was once so dense that it would hobble (trip and entangle) any deer trying to walk through it. See also Dog Hobble Branch.

Defeat Ridge Thunderhead Mt., NC/TN m-w-nw-n ❧ 1. See Bote Mountain for one name origin theory. 2. Another explanation concerns Col. Return J. Meigs (see Meigs Mountain), an early surveyor, who admitted he was defeated in trying to climb this peak.

Den Branch Cove Creek Gap, NC sw **Den Ridge** Dellwood, NC n-nw ❧ 1. The ridge was named for a huge den of rattlesnakes. 2. It was named for the presence of the lair (den) of some other kind of animal. Perhaps it was a panther, as evidenced by Panther Spring Gap, just to the northeast.

Derrick Knob, Derrick Knob Spring Thunderhead Mt., NC/TN e ❧ 1. Named for a Derrick family that moved into Sevier County, Tennessee, prior to 1807. They acquired their property through a land grant in 1807, as a result of their occupancy there. 2. Named for a man called Derrick, who built a cabin in this area circa 1880. The Derrick Knob and Big Chestnut Bald areas were at one time called Hall Cabin, for a prominent home in the area. See Hall Cabin.

Desolation Branch Thunderhead Mt., NC/TN m-s-e ❧ 1. Named for an incident that occurred along this stream in the 1880s. Three men were caught in a snowstorm while hunting here, and were forced to make camp. During the night a boot of one of the men was placed too close to the fire and burned up. Another of the party cut the top off of one of his boots and made a sort of moccasin that got the bootless man home. Thereafter, that stream was called Desolation Branch in remembrance of the incident. 2. Named for its rugged, dense growth of rhododendron and mountain laurel, and its sheer cliffs and ledges. Also has been called Lanky Branch.

Devil Branch Silers Bald, NC/TN e **Devils Den** Mt. Guyot, TN/NC nw **Devils Nest Creek** Thunderhead Mt., TN/NC n-nw **etc.** ❧ The use of the word devil (hell, purgatory, etc.) in place names in the mountains denotes a rugged and desperate landscape. It was generally given to places that only the Devil himself could negotiate or would want to spend time in. These were places where any form of agriculture was out of the question and places where one could become hopelessly confused or lost. In short, they were bad lands—worthless places to be avoided.

Devils Bench Thunderhead Mt., NC/TN m-n **Devils Branch** Thunderhead Mt., NC/TN ne ❧ See Devils Courthouse.

Devils Chute Gatlinburg, TN w ***n.l.*** ❧ Named for a deep, steep-sided ravine west of, and parallel to, Laurel Falls Trail, through which Laurel Creek loudly rushes.

Devils Courthouse Thunderhead Mt., NC/TN m **Devils Courthouse Branch** Thunderhead Mt., NC/TN m-e ***n.l.*** **Devils Courthouse Ridge** Silers Bald, NC/TN se-e ❧ After becoming lost in this area, and almost dying, while conducting a survey of the Cherokee Indian boundary in 1797, Col. Return J. Meigs (see Meigs Mountain) named this ridge the Devils Courthouse to commemorate his struggles. Furthermore, because he felt he had been judged by the Devil himself, a spur of that same ridge he named Devils Bench, a place where the Devil might have been sitting while judging Meigs.

Doe Knob, Doe Ridge Cades Cove, TN/NC s ❧ Named for a female deer. It is adjacent to Buck Gap, which was named for a male deer.

Dog Hobble Branch Thunderhead Mt., NC/TN ne ❧ Named for the evergreen shrub dog-hobble (*Leucothoe fontanesiana*) that grows in impenetrable thickets along this stream. In pre-park days, bears would escape the hunting dogs by running through such obstacles. The bears were big enough to leap over it, but it would hobble (trip and entrap) the dogs. Sometimes the bears would then turn on the dogs and crush them.

Dome Falls Mt. Le Conte, TN/NC m ❧ Named for the unique half-dome shape of the spray and water of this falls as it tumbles over a crescent-shaped rock shelf. Unfortunately, this falls is active only during times of very wet weather.

Dorsey Branch Wear Cove, TN s ***n.l.*** **Dorsey Gap** Wear Cove, TN sw ❧ Named in honor of Civil War veteran Anderson Dorsey, whose property was to the west of the gap which bears his name.

Double Gap #1 Cove Creek Gap, NC nw **Double Gap #2, Double Gap Branch** Dellwood, NC w **Double Gap Ridge** Dellwood, NC w-nw ❧ Named for the close proximity of dual gaps at these sites.

Double Mountain Kinzel Springs, TN s-se ❧ So named because it has twin (double) peaks.

Double Spring Branch Silers Bald, NC/TN m-n ***n.l.*** **Double Spring Gap** Silers Bald, NC/TN m-e ❧ So named because this gap has two springs situated about 50 feet apart. One drains north to the Little River and the other south to the Tuckaseegee River. Their waters eventually reunite, in the Tennessee River, 100 miles to the west.

Double Trestle Branch Thunderhead Mt., NC/TN ne ❧ This name is left over from the 1920s logging railroad era, when two trestles (railroad bridges) crossed this stream near its confluence with Indian Flats Prong.

Drinklog Branch Noland Creek, NC ne ❧ A log once fell across a section of this steep rocky stream and impounded a small pool. As luck would have it, the pool formed in such a way that one could ride a horse up next to it, lean over, and get a drink without dismounting.

Dripping Spring Mountain Silers Bald, NC/TN nw ➧ Named for the ledges along the flanks of this mountain where water oozes and drips from crevices. This mountain, and adjacent Bent Arm, were once called Long Arm.

Dry Sluice [Branch] Mt. Guyot, TN/NC sw ***n.l.*** **Dry Sluice Gap** Mt. Guyot, TN/NC sw ➧ 1. Named for a small hollow or valley called a sluice, which has a spring-fed stream that sinks beneath the surface for several hundred yards before reemerging. Hence, the upper part of the sluice is generally dry. 2. This name may also be linked to the early logging industry, when logs were sluiced (moved down the mountain) from timber cutting operations.

Dude Branch Cove Creek Gap, NC w ➧ Named for Dude Hannah, who lived near this stream, and was notorious for his moonshining activities. Formerly called Messer Branch.

Dunn Creek Jones Cove, TN se ➧ Named for a Dunn family that once settled along this stream. Probably related to the Dunn families of Cades and Tuckaleechee coves.

Eagle Rocks Mt. Guyot, TN/NC s **Eagle Rocks Prong** Mt. Guyot, TN/NC m-s ➧ Named for a rocky ledge that looks like the lair of an eagle. Golden and bald eagles inhabit the park, though both are uncommon.

Easy Ridge Clingmans Dome, NC/TN s ➧ Thought to be a satirical reference to this ridge, since walking across it is anything but easy.

Ecoah Branch Fontana Dam, NC ne ➧ 1. Name is a shortened version of Stecoah, a township in Graham County, North Carolina, south of Fontana Lake. Stecoah is derived from the Cherokee term stika'yi, meaning lean, as in a shortage of game. 2. Name is a variation of Ecola, a former community in Swain County, North Carolina, now under the waters of Fontana Lake.

Edens Garden Creek Thunderhead Mt., NC/TN nw-n ❥ A name inspired by the Old Testament Garden of Eden. There is quite a contrast between this heavenly designation and the next stream up the West Prong of the Little River, which is Devils Nest Creek.

Ekaneetlee Branch Cades Cove, TN/NC s-m **Ekaneetlee Creek** Cades Cove, TN/NC s-se **Ekaneetlee Gap*** Cades Cove, TN/NC s ❥ 1. The word Ekaneetlee is a corruption of the Cherokee term Egwanulti, meaning towns by the river. 2. Another source states that Egwanulti may also mean old spicewood in Cherokee. 3. It may also be a Cherokee term for a low gap. In fact, Ekaneetlee Gap is the lowest point on the Smoky Mountain crest and the site of an ancient Cherokee trail that once connected Indian settlements on either side of the Smokies. *Formerly called Opossum Gap and Equonettly. Also spelled Egkenatly and Equinulty. See also Oconaluftee River.

Elkmont Gatlinburg, TN s-sw ❥ Prior to the purchase of this area by the Little River Lumber Company, members of the Knoxville, Tennessee, Elks Club (a men's benevolent and social fraternity) had big summer gatherings here. This gave rise to the name Elk Mountain that was later shortened to Elkmont. This once

The Elks and the Rebeccas on their annual picnic at Elkmont

thriving community was initially called Tarpaper Camp, shortly after it was established by the Little River Lumber Company. Early membership in the Wonderland (Hotel) private club included a lot in the Elkmont area, upon which members were welcome to build a vacation cabin. Many constructed such cabins in the 1920s.

The 80 that remain now lie abandoned since the National Park Service condemned them and took the land back as per written agreements enacted when the park was established in 1934. See Wonderland Hotel.

Elliott Cove Branch, Elliott Improvement* Clingmans Dome, NC/TN se-s ***n.l.*** ❥ Named for one of the Elliott families that acquired land grants in the Smokies as early as 1837. *A one and one-half mile stretch of good, flat, once-cultivated land along Elliott Cove Branch. See also Pierce Improvement.

El rado Kinzel Springs, TN s ***n.l.*** **El rado Creek** Kinzel Springs, TN s-se ***n.l.*** ❥ After returning from the gold fields of California in 1847, Dr. Calvin Post prospected for gold here. He named this area El Dorado, meaning "the golden." Gold was never found here, though some of the open mine pits are still visible from the Rich Mountain Road. This is one of only two non-American and non-Indian place names in the park. The other is Peruvian Branch. See also Post Spring.

Wesley Enloe, son of Abraham

Emerts Cove Mt. Le Conte, TN/NC n-ne ❥ Named for a Frederick S. Emert family that acquired a land grant in this area in the 1790s. They were one of the original settlers in the Greenbrier Cove area. Frederick was a Methodist minister.

Enloe Creek Mt. Guyot, TN/NC s **Enloe Hollow Branch** Mt. Le Conte, TN/NC m **Enloe Ridge** Smokemont, NC ne **Enloe Slave Cemetery** Smokemont, NC s ❥ Named for the family of Abraham and Wes Enloe, 1804 settlers in the Oconaluftee region. Abraham, who developed a farm and trading business in the area, is alleged to have been the father of Abraham Lincoln.

Fairfax Community Fontana Dam, NC w ❧ 1. A former community named for the Fax or Fairfax family that once lived in the area. The Fax name is still associated with place names in adjacent Graham County, North Carolina. 2. Named for a mulatto man named Fair Fax. He received the name because he had a light complexion.

Falling Rock Creek Luftee Knob, NC/TN s-se ❧ Named for an incident that occurred near Lost Bottom Creek in the early 1920s. Two men spending the night under a rock ledge built a fire to keep warm. During the night, the heat of the fire caused a large rock slab to break loose and fall from the overhang, fatally crushing a Mr. Camel (see Camel Gap).

Baskins Creek Falls

Falls Branch Mt. Le Conte, TN/NC w ❧ Named for picturesque Baskins Creek Falls which is located near the mouth of this stream.

False Gap Mt. Guyot, TN/NC sw **False Gap Prong** Mt. Guyot, TN/NC w-sw **False Gap Spring** Mt. Guyot, TN/NC sw ❧ The name probably refers to the Porters Gap Sag, which is not much of a gap.

Feezell Branch Cades Cove, TN/NC n ❧ Named for a Feezell family that settled in Cades Cove prior to 1861, but did not receive a land grant until 1870.

Fighting Creek Gatlinburg, TN m-e **Fighting Creek Gap** Gatlinburg, TN m ❧ 1. Named for a long battle or argument by locals concerning the location of a school house along this stream. 2. Two mountain men, a Cole and an Owenby, had an argument and almost fought one another along this stream. 3. Local boys would fight here for sport on weekends. 4. The school house here was used as a temporary courthouse, and after court, if not satisfied with the decision, the loser settled the score by fighting the winner here. 5. Two men started to fight here, one made a joke, both started laughing, apologies were made, and they made up.

Finley Cane Trail* *n.s.*, Finley Cove, Finley Cove Creek Thunderhead Mt., NC/TN nw ❧ Probably named for a Finley family that acquired land grants in Blount County, Tennessee, as early as 1778. *A patch of river cane is still found along this trail. See also Canebreak Branch.

Fire Cherry Branch Silers Bald, NC/TN n ❧ Named for the pin cherry (*Prunus pensylvanica*), a small tree that is often called fire cherry because it invades burned-over areas in almost pure stands. The name of this branch and its sister stream, Ash Camp Branch, indicate previous forest fire damage in the area.

Firescald Branch Wear Cove, TN sw **Firescald Ridge** Silers Bald, NC/TN m-s ❧ "Firescald" probably refers to forest fire damage in this area.

First Branch Gatlinburg, TN s-se ❧ This name is related to Second Branch and Third Branch, all adjacent tributaries on Little River.

Fish Camp Prong Silers Bald, NC/TN n-ne-w-m ❧ Named for a fishing and hunting reserve in this area that was called the Fish Camp. This area had always been a popular and productive fishing site, and also gave its name to a former Little River Lumber Company logging camp.

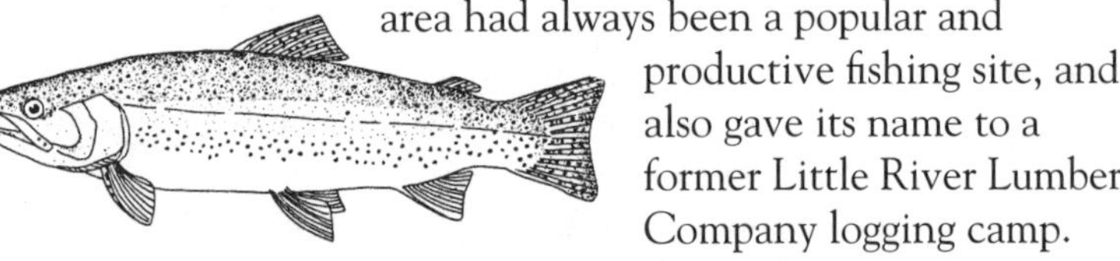

Fittified Spring Mt. Le Conte, TN/NC e ❧ This name is descriptive of an intermittent spring that is low, or dry, at times and free flowing at others. In other words, it is fitful or characterized by irregular bursts of activity. After an earthquake in 1916, it was said to have a seven minute on, seven minute off flow pattern. However, a dynamite blast during Civilian Conservation Corps (CCC) trail construction in 1936 interrupted its regular pattern. Thereafter, it became irregular, or fittified. This spring was earlier called the Spasmodic Spring, for the same reason.

Front porch of the Walker Sisters' home.

Five Sisters Cove Wear Cove, TN e *n.l.* ❧ Named for the five Walker sisters, the spinster daughters of pioneer John Walker. They resisted eviction by the National Park Service and continued to live in Little Greenbrier Cove after park establishment. Their names were Hettie, Louisa, Martha, Polly, and Margaret. The last of the sisters, Louisa, died in 1964. Their home and some outbuildings still stand in this cove. Formerly called Little Greenbrier Cove.

Flats, The Blockhouse, TN se ❧ The name applies to an area of level ground between the park boundary and Chilhowee Mountain.

Flint Branch Wear Cove, TN sw-s **Flint Gap #1*** Calderwood, TN/NC m **Flint Gap #2** Fontana Dam, NC ne **Flint Rock Branch** Gatlinburg, TN se **Flint Rock Cove** Luftee Knob, NC/TN ne **Flint Spring Gap** Thunderhead Mt., NC/TN sw ❧ Named for hard, fine-grained, quartzite rock called flint that is found in these areas. Because it could be chipped and honed to a very sharp edge, the early Indians used this rock to make projectile points (arrowheads), stone knives, axes, and other tools. *Allegedly, there was an old Indian flint quarry in this area, possibly along what is now the Hannah Mountain Trail.

Fodderstack Branch ***n.l.*****, Fodderstack Mountain** Wear Cove, TN s **Fodderstack Rock** Thunderhead Mt., NC/TN w ***n.s.*** ❧ Named for this peak's resemblance to a mound of coarsely chopped livestock feed (corn, corn stalks, hay, etc.) piled around a pole like a haystack in a field. See also Shuckstack Ridge.

Fodderstack

Fontana Lake Bryson City, NC w **Fontana Old Town*** Fontana Dam, NC e ❧ Named for the Montvale Lumber Company town of Fontana. 1. The name was supposedly made-up by the wife of the lumber company executive vice-president because the U.S. Postal Service insisted that it have one. According to her, it was an area of lovely flowering glens and waterfalls that looked like fountains leaping from ledge to ledge. Probably derived from the Italian word for fountain. 2. A second source states that Fontana is an Indian word meaning, "at the foot of the mountain." Which Native American language it is from is unknown. 3. Another source states that the name was derived from Montana, a mineral rich state. Such a name may have been aimed at attracting investors to potential untapped mineral resources of North Carolina. 4. Still another source states that it was named for an Italian naturalist, Felice Fontana, who visited this area in the 1700s. *Originally called Fairfax (see Fairfax community).

Forge Creek* Cades Cove, TN/NC sw-m-w-nw **Forge Creek Spring** Cades Cove, TN/NC w ♣ Named for a bloomery forge, once operated by Daniel Davis Foute, on this creek. In ironworking terms, a bloomery is a puddling furnace or forge in which charcoal, iron ore and limestone (which acts as a catalyst) are combined to produce wrought iron blooms or metal bars. These bars are then further processed (by blacksmiths) into iron implements like horseshoes. This was the site of the earliest forge operated in Blount County, Tennessee (1826–1846). It predates the Foute Bloomery in Cades Cove (see Forge Knob). *Formerly called Marion Creek, in honor of Marion Burchfield, a local resident.

Forge Knob Cades Cove, TN/NC sw **Forge Knob Branch** Cades Cove, TN/NC sw ♣ Named for the Cades Cove (Fonte) Bloomery Forge that operated here from 1827 to 1847. See also Forge Creek.

Forney Creek* Noland Creek, NC m-n **Forney Creek Cascade** Silers Bald, NC/TN e *n.s.* **Forney Ridge** Clingmans Dome, NC/TN sw-w ♣
1. Named for Jacob Forney who settled in this area circa 1750, at the junction of his namesake stream and the Tuckaseegee River. The old home site is now under the waters of Fontana Lake.
2. Named for an old man Forney who fell in this creek and drowned. *Former site of a fish hatchery and rearing ponds that produced trout for stocking park streams in the 1930s.

Forrester Ridge Thunderhead Mt., NC/TN sw-w-m-s ♣ Named for a Forrester family that settled in the Hazel Creek area in the late 1800s.

Fort Harry Mt. Le Conte, TN/NC sw ♣ 1. Named for earthworks (fort or blockhouse) hastily-erected near the Chimney Tops during the Civil War. It was constructed to protect Federal troops who were building a road to Alum Cave and was named for a Harry (last name unknown), one of the soldiers who helped construct it.
2. An African-American man named Harry had a camp at a stream crossing near this area, and Fort Harry is actually Ford Harry, a shallow place where people forded or crossed the steam. See also Alum Cave.

Fountain Branch Smokemont, NC ne ❧ Formerly called Big Spring Branch, which may explain the name fountain, especially when the water level is high.

Fox Branch #1,* Fox Branch #2** Fontana Dam, NC nw-w *n.l.* ❧ *Formerly Fax Branch. **Flows through the old town of Fairfax and may have formerly been associated with the name Fax, rather than Fox.

Frowning Rock Prong Mt. Guyot, TN/NC sw-s ❧ Thought to be named for a nearby rock formation that resembles a frowning face.

G

Garretts Gap Bunches Bald, NC e ❧ Named for William Garrett, a land owner and resident in the Pigeon River Valley and later Ivy Hill and Jonathan Creek townships.

Gatlinburg Trail Gatlinburg, TN e *n.l.* ❧ Named for the city of Gatlinburg, which was named for Radford Gatlin: 1. A local merchant who kept the town's post office in his store in the mid 1850s. 2. An unpopular Confederate sympathizer who agreed to leave town under the condition that the town be named for him. The town was formerly called Whiteoak Flats. This trail runs from Sugarlands Visitor Center to the Gatlinburg city limits.

Gatlinburg, TN

Georges Branch Clingmans Dome, NC/TN se ❧ 1. George was a slang expression for cocaine, a drug used by many of the early loggers in the Smokies. The stream name may relate to this term. 2. The stream may also have been named for a man or boy, or it may have been the surname of a family unknown.

Gilliland Creek Cove Creek Gap, NC w ❧ Named for a John Gilliland family who settled in this area in the 1790s.

Glades, The Thunderhead Mt., NC/TN m ***n.l.*** **Glady Branch** Noland Creek, NC m-n ❧ A glade is an open space in a forest, or an area of clumped or sparse woody vegetation.

Goldmine Branch #1* Noland Creek, NC m-n **Goldmine Branch #2** Mt. Guyot, TN/NC sw ***n.l.*** **Gold Mine Gap** Blockhouse, TN se ❧ Named for actual or legendary gold mines or gold mining in these areas. See El rado. *This stream was not named for the presence of a gold mine, but rather for the hope of finding one, after a small quantity of gold was found in drillings along Eagle Creek a dozen miles to the west.

Gorges, The Smokemont, NC ne ❧ A boulder-ridden, tunnel-like canyon or river gorge along a section of Raven Fork.

Goshen Prong Silers Bald, NC/TN n-m-e **Goshen Prong Valley, Goshen Ridge** Silers Bald, NC/TN n-ne-e ❧ Goshen refers to a fertile land. According to the Bible, Goshen was the fertile land assigned to the Israelites in Egypt.

Grapeyard Branch Mt. Le Conte, TN/NC n **Grapeyard Ridge** Mt. Le Conte, TN/NC m-n-ne ❧ Named for the profuse growth of wild grape (*Vitis* sp.) vines in these areas, or named for places adjacent to them. In some parts of the Great Smoky Mountains grape vines grow so thick they tear down standing trees and create natural openings in the forest.

Grass Branch Luftee Knob, NC/TN sw **Grassy Branch** Gatlinburg, TN e **Grassy Flats** Calderwood, TN/NC s ❧ Probably named for open patches of grasses and sedges in these areas. These areas were probably maintained as pasture or cultivated in pre-park days.

Grassy Patch Mt. Le Conte, TN/NC s ❧ Name describes the grassy glade at the head of the Alum Cave Trail to Mount Le Conte. Grassy patches were often cultivated beneath trees and along streams and ridges. Whether this site is natural or originally cultivated is not known. Grassy Patch is now the site of Alum Cave Parking Area.

Grayback Branch Wear Cove, TN e ❧ Named for the presence of what mountain folk called graybacks—rounded, boulder-sized, gray colored, lichen and moss encrusted rocks.

Gray Wolf Creek Noland Creek, NC n ❧ Named for the gray or timber wolf (*Canis lupus*) that once lived in the Smokies. The last authentic account of a gray wolf in the Smokies was in 1900.

The Great Smoky Mountains

Great Smoky Mountains ❧ Named for the misty blue-gray haze that hangs over these mountains much of the year. This haze is the result of great quantities of moisture in the air. This moisture, plus trace chemicals, is given off by the lush vegetation, or evaporated from soils and running water. The first known reference to this name was in 1789, as part of a boundary description, when North Carolina ceded its western lands to the federal government for inclusion in the Territory of the United States South of the River Ohio. The description read in part, ". . . and hence along the highest ridge of the said mountain to the place where it is called Great Iron or Smoaky (sic) Mountain. . . ." To the Cherokees, the mountains were called Sha-cona-ga, meaning "blue, like smoke." The Cherokee also called them unica, which means white. From this Cherokee term comes Unaka and Unicoi, which are the names of sister mountain ranges to the northeast and southwest, respectively. Formerly called Great Iron Mountain.

Great Smoky Mountains Institute at Tremont Wear Cove, TN s *n.l.* ❧ This environmental education center occupies the site of old Camp (Margaret) Townsend. See Townsend "Y."

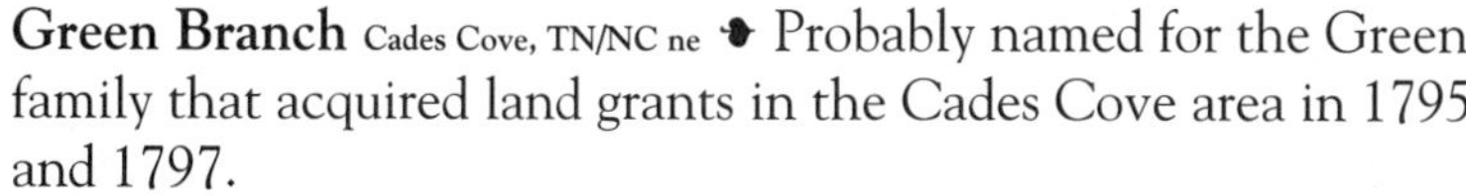

Green Branch Cades Cove, TN/NC ne ❧ Probably named for the Green family that acquired land grants in the Cades Cove area in 1795 and 1797.

Greenbrier Cove* Mt. Le Conte, TN/NC ne-e **Greenbrier Creek** Hartford, TN/NC sw **Greenbrier Pinnacle**** Mt. Guyot, TN/NC nw-n-ne ❧ Named for a woody, climbing vine (*Smilax* sp.), with green photosynthetic stems and heavy thorns. Sometimes called carrion flower because of its foul-smelling blossoms that attract carrion flies. Also called saw brier because of its formidable thorns. It often occurs in almost impenetrable thickets called brierlicks. Three species of brier occur in the park. *Formerly called Brier Cove. Believed to have been settled by a Whaley family in the early 1800s, hence another name, Whaley Settlement. **Formerly called Pinnacle (see glossary).

Greer Branch* Cades Cove, TN/NC s **Greer Knob** Cades Cove, TN/NC s ❧ Named for Andy Greer, one of the first settlers in Cades Cove. He lost 15–20 head of cattle on his namesake knob in a lightning storm around the turn of the century. *This same stream is called Green Branch on the Fontana, NC, USGS topo map.

Gregory Bald* Cades Cove, TN/NC sw **Gregory Ridge**** Cades Cove, TN/NC sw-w ❧ Named for Russell Gregory (1795–1864) and his wife Susan, believed to be the third white family to settle in the Cades Cove area. The couple settled on Gregory Bald in the 1820s and raised livestock. They later moved down to Cades Cove. D. D. Foute, John Coffin, Richard Wilson, and Gregory jointly purchased 1,550 acres of mountain land, including his namesake bald, in 1853. He was also one of the developers of the failed Parson's Turnpike (see Parson Bald), in the late 1830s, and lived at Rich Gap for a while. Russell Gregory lost his life during the Civil War at the hands of North Carolina Confederate raiders. *The Cherokee called this site *Tsistugi*, meaning the Rabbit Place. It was home to Little Rabbit who was the chief of their clan. Formerly called Great Bald (central peak near the Little Tennessee) by Professor Guyot (see Mount Guyot). Also formerly called Big Bald. (See glossary for term bald.) **Formerly called Fork Ridge.

Joe Gregory

Gregory Cave Cades Cove, TN/NC n ❧ Named for Joe Gregory, a former owner of the cave. It was once a commercial attraction, opened in July of 1925. A small Delco generator once furnished electricity to light the cave. Some deteriorating bridges and walkways can still be seen in the cave, where, in 1935, visitors paid 50 cents for a tour. For a time the cave was the site of Saturday night hoedowns with live music and dancing. Some say the cave was also a good place to hide moonshine from revenuers. It has been called Gregorys Cave. (Note: a permit is required to enter all park caves.)

Grotto Falls Mt. Le Conte, TN/NC m ❧ Named for the presence of an overhanging bluff, or grotto, behind this waterfall. Formerly known as Dome Falls (but not to be mistaken for the Dome Falls located near it).

Groundhog Branch Gatlinburg, TN se-s ❧ 1. Named for a piece of machinery called a groundhog or groundhog skidder, used in logging operations. It employs cables to move logs along the ground. 2. May have been named for the animal. See Groundhog Creek.

Groundhog skidder

Groundhog Creek, Groundhog Ridge Hartford, TN/NC s-se ❧ 1. Probably named for the groundhog (*Marmota monax*), a large and stocky member of the rodent family, also know as a woodchuck or whistlepig. 2. However, it might have been named for the groundhog skidder. See Groundhog Branch.

Gulf Prong Mt. Guyot, TN/NC s ❧ A gulf in the mountain vernacular is a deep, wide valley, gorge, or hollow.

Gunlock Ridge Tuskeegee, NC n ❧ A gunlock is the locking mechanism on a rifle. It secures the hammer and locks it in place. This ridge may resemble a gunlock in profile, or someone could have lost or found one there.

Gunna Creek Thunderhead Mt., NC/TN sw-w **Gunnagee Branch** Mt. Guyot, TN/NC ne ❧ Gunna is the Cherokee term for turkey (*Meleagris gallopavo*), a large native bird frequently sought by hunters.

Gunter Branch Noland Creek, NC w-nw **Gunter Fork** Luftee Knob, NC/TN n-w-m **Gunter Fork Falls** Luftee Knob, NC/TN m *n.s.* ❧ Probably named for a Gunter family, early residents of the Big Creek area.

Guyot Spur Mt. Guyot, TN/NC m-e ❧ See Mt. Guyot.

Half Acre Ridge Cove Creek Gap, NC s-sw ❧ 1. Name may be related to Hells Half Acre Branch and may have previously been known as Hells Half Acre Ridge, for its rough terrain. See Devil Branch. 2. Name could be a corruption of Huffaker, for a Huffaker family that once lived in the area.

Hall Branch Cove Creek Gap, NC sw-s ❧ Probably named for a Hall family that settled in Haywood County, North Carolina circa 1800.

Hall Cabin Thunderhead Mt., NC/TN s ❧ Named for local settler Jesse Crayton "Crate" or "Crede" Hall who constructed the building as a herder cabin. He moved his family into the structure in 1877. J. H. Kress, of New York City department store fame, built a luxury hunting lodge just to the south of the Hall Cabin in the 1920s. The lodge burned in 1960.

Hammer mill

Hammer Branch Bryson City, NC n ❧ Probably named for the presence of a pounding or hammer mill on this stream. Hammer mills pulverized corn by pounding and breaking it up, rather than by grinding it between mill stones, as was the case with tub and overshot mills. Pounding mills were used by the Cherokee Indians and adopted by early European settlers.

Hannah Branch Calderwood, TN/NC m-e-ne ❧ See Hannah Mountain.

Hannah Mountain Calderwood, TN/NC ne-e-m-se ❧ Named for the Milton Hannah family that settled in this area in the 1830s or 1840s.

Hant Hollow Silers Bald, NC/TN ne *n.l.* ❧ The word "hant" is haunt in the mountain vernacular. Apparently this name arose from the feeling that this hollow is haunted.

Happy Valley* Calderwood, TN/NC n **Happy Valley Gap** Calderwood, TN/NC nw **Happy Valley Ridge** Blockhouse, TN s ❧ This valley was named by families who moved here from another Happy Valley in Carter County, Tennessee. The name is descriptive of a peaceful, bucolic valley nestled between two mountains. *Formerly called Rhea Valley in honor of Robert Rhea, a Revolutionary War and Indian War veteran who died here in 1850.

Hatcher Mountain Blockhouse, TN se ❥ Believed to be named for Alex Hatcher, who settled in nearby Hatcher Flats, where a residential development called Top of the World is presently located.

Haw Gap Thunderhead Mt., NC/TN w **Haw Gap Branch** Thunderhead Mt., NC/TN w-sw-s **Haw Gap Spring** Thunderhead Mt., NC/TN w ❥ Sometime in the 1850s a person asked directions on how to get over Jenkins Trail Ridge and into Cades Cove. The person was told to turn haw (or left) at this gap. Haw is an old plowman's command for a horse or mule to turn left. Gee is the command for a right turn.

Haywood County, North Carolina ❥ Named for John Haywood of Raleigh, a North Carolina State Treasurer (1787–1827). The county seat is Waynesville.

Hazel Creek Fontana Dam, NC e **Hazel Creek Cascades** Silers Bald, NC/TN w-m ❥ Named for the American hazel (*Corylus americana*) a shrubby plant that often forms thickets. It is one of the first plants to bloom in the spring, often flowering in February, or even January.

Heintooga Overlook

Heintooga Bald Bunches Bald, NC m **Heintooga Ridge** Bunches Bald, NC m-w **Heintooga Overlook** Bunches Bald, NC m ❥ The word Heintooga is a corruption of the Cherokee I-yen-too-ga, meaning hiding place or refuge, or more literally, a dwelling in the wilderness or an inhabitant of the wilderness. Visible from the Heintooga Overlook is a vast wilderness, some of which was the last refuge of the Cherokees trying to avoid being expelled from their homeland in the 1830s along the infamous Trail of Tears.

Hell Ridge Luftee Knob, NC/TN n-nw *n.s.* ❧ This area was logged in 1924, and later a four-mile section was burned and eroded to the point that locals referred to it as Hell Ridge.

Hells Half Acre Branch Cove Creek Gap, NC s *n.s.* ❧ This name is believed to relate to the very rough terrain in this area. See also Devil Branch.

Hemlock Knob Silers Bald, NC/TN w ❧ Named for its dense growth of Eastern hemlock trees (*Tsuga canadensis*).

Hemphill Bald Dellwood, NC w ❧ Named for Thomas Hemphill who settled in Haywood County, North Carolina, in 1792. He is believed to have constructed Haywood County's first grist mill on his namesake creek to the east of what is today the national park. See glossary for bald.

Henderson Branch Gatlinburg, TN se **Henderson Prong** Wear Cove, TN se ❧ Most likely named for a Henderson family that settled in what is now the park in the late 1700s or early 1800s. Perhaps it was William Henderson and his wife Mary who acquired land grants in Wear Valley in 1808 and 1810.

Hen Wallow Creek Hartford, TN/NC sw **Hen Wallow Falls** Hartford, TN/NC sw *n.s.* ❧ Named for the Ruffed Grouse or wood hen and its habit of wallowing and stirring up dust in patches of dry soil. 2. Another account suggests that Henwallow was a grudge name given to this community by another, after the people of Henwallow nicknamed the other community Roostertown. The name Roostertown allegedly came about when one of its citizens ordered 100 baby chickens by mail. The buyer expected to get mostly hens (females), but received 95 roosters.

Hermit Branch Clingmans Dome, NC/TN m ❧ 1. Possibly named for an old man who once lived in solitude along this stream. 2. Possibly named for a bird, the Hermit Thrush (*Catharus guttatus*) that lives in the park.

Hesse Creek Kinzel Springs, TN sw ❧ Named for a John Hesse (or Hess), a Swiss immigrant, who once lived in the Millers Cove area, adjacent to what is now the park. He moved to this location from Carter County, Tennessee.

Hickory King Branch Gatlinburg, TN se ❧ 1. Probably named for Hickory King, a variety of corn that could have been planted in the flat areas along this stream. 2. Possibly named for a King family that once lived in this area, with the first part of the name referring to the numerous hickory trees (*Carya* sp.) along this stream.

Hickory Turn Branch, Hickory Turn Ridge Calderwood, TN/NC ne-e ❧ The hickory part of these names refers to the hickory trees (*Carya* sp.) so prevalent in this area. Turn refers to the fact that Andy McCully Ridge makes an abrupt 90 degree turn at its southwest end, thus producing a northwest spur called Hickory Turn Ridge. The stream is named for the ridge.

High Rocks Noland Creek, NC nw ❧ Named for a tumbled mass of rocks, some larger than a house. Probably one of the park's several block (boulder) fields created during a recent ice age.

High Rocks fire tower

High Top Mt. Le Conte, TN/NC s ❧ Named for the highest central peak of Mount Le Conte. This point, on the three-summited mountain, was originally named Mount Le Conte by Professor S. B. Buckley, who explored the area in 1858 (see Mount Buckley). He originally named the peak to the west Mount Curtis and the one to the east Mount Stafford.

Hills Creek Mt. Le Conte, TN/NC n ❧ Named for a Hill family that settled in this area.

Hogan Hollow Kinzel Springs, TN sw ❧ Probably named for a Hogan family that once lived in this area.

Holy Butt Gatlinburg, TN m ❧ Probably named for Holy Branch, a stream that arises on its southeast flank. A woman called Aunt Lydia lived on this stream that was originally called Holly Branch. She changed the name to Holy Branch, thinking the new name more fitting. Hence the name of the stream and the name of its adjacent peak (butt). See butt in glossary. Formerly called Holly Butt.

Honey Cove Branch Wear Cove, TN s-se ❧ Probably named for the presence of one or more wild bee trees along this stream. Early settlers would have collected the honey from such trees and perhaps transferred the bees to a bee gum (or domestic hive) near their home. Also known as Copperhead Cove Branch.

Hornet Tree Top Thunderhead Mt., NC/TN n ❧ Name is probably in reference to a hornet's nest in a tree on this peak. Bald-face hornets (*Vespula maculata*) build large, gray, paper nests, often larger than basketballs.

Horse Pen Ridge Dellwood, NC nw ❧ Makeshift or temporary corrals were sometimes constructed by hunters, herders, and other travelers by downing trees and arranging limbs and trunks to create temporary brushy enclosures. Such enclosures were called horse pens and probably account for this place name.

Horseshoe, The Tuskeegee, NC nw-n ❧ This giant amphitheater-like structure is shaped like a gargantuan horseshoe around a horseshoe bend of Hazel Creek.

Horsetrough Ridge Bunches Bald, NC m-w-s **Horsetrough Ridge Overlook** Bunches Bald, NC s ❧ Said to be named for two (or three) horse feed troughs, hollowed out of a basswood tree in the 1800s by a cattle herder named Jonathan Creek. Although he planned to return and take them home, he never did and they just rotted there beside the old trail. Another source places the carved horse troughs at the overlook, not on the ridge. The overlook provides a panoramic view of the ridge and surrounding area.

Hostility Branch Silers Bald, NC/TN n ❥ This small stream is located near Battle Branch in Battle Hollow. The two streams are alleged to have been named for the fact that the country was so rough and hostile, you had to battle your way through it. War Branch is also located just downstream.

Huggins Branch* Silers Bald, NC/TN sw **Huggins Creek** Silers Bald, NC/TN se-s-m-e **Huggins Ridge** Silers Bald, NC/TN sw ❥ Named for a Huggins family that settled in the Hazel Creek area in the 1800s. *Formerly called Big Huggin Branch and Big Higgens Branch.

Huggins Hell Mt. Le Conte, TN/NC s ❥ 1. Folklore has it that a man by the name of Huggins decided one day that he would explore this area of lush, seemingly impenetrable vegetation, "If he had to go to hell itself to do it." Since he is said to have never returned, it is assumed that he went to hell trying. 2. This dense growth of mountain laurel and rhododendron was discovered by, and named for, a man named Huggins.

Hughes Ridge Mt. Guyot, TN/NC s ❥ 1. Named in honor of Rafe Hughes and his wife Lizzie, who settled in the Oconaluftee River Valley in the early 1800s. 2. Named for Ralph and Sarah Hughes who settled in the area circa 1795.

Hurricane Branch Cades Cove, TN/NC se **Hurricane Creek*** Bunches Bald, NC ne **Hurricane Mountain**** Kinzel Springs, TN w-sw **Hurricane Ridge** Cades Cove, TN/NC se ❥ Many mountain people refer to tornadoes or heavy wind storms as hurricanes, hence the origin of these place names. *Name may relate to a circa 1898 severe thunderstorm or tornado that caused damage along this stream or it may just be descriptive of its turbulent behavior when in flood. **Named for a windstorm or tornado that damaged vegetation in the area in the early 1800s.

Huskey Branch Falls

Huskey Branch, Huskey Branch Falls Gatlinburg, TN s *n.s.* **Huskey Creek** Clingmans Dome, NC/TN ne **Huskey Gap** Gatlinburg, TN se ❥ Named for descendants of the James Wesley Huskey family, one of the original families to settle in the Smokies in the 1800s. At the time the government purchased the land for the park, 38 parcels in Sevier County, Tennessee, alone were owned by Huskeys.

Hyatt Bald Luftee Knob, NC/TN sw **Hyatt Branch** Noland Creek, NC m-n **Hyatt Creek*** Bunches Bald, NC nw **Hyatt Lane**** Cades Cove, TN/NC n) **Hyatt Ridge** Luftee Knob, NC/TN sw ❥ These places were named for Hyatt families that lived throughout the Smokies before park establishment. The Hyatts were among the first white settlers in Haywood County, North Carolina in the 1780s. *Named specifically for Edward (Ned) Hyatt who cleared land along this stream and probably grazed cattle on the nearby bald that also bears his name. **Named for one of the first families to settle in Cades Cove. By the 1840s they had left the cove and migrated to Missouri.

Icewater Spring Mt. Le Conte, TN/NC se ❥ Located at an elevation of nearly 6,000 feet, the water from this spring is indeed chilly. See Coldspring Branch.

Improvement Branch Silers Bald, NC/TN nw-n *n.l.* ❥ Improvement is a term once used to indicate the cultivation of land or construction of one or more structures on it.

Inadu Creek, Inadu Knob,* Inadu Mountain Luftee Knob, NC/TN nw ❧ Inadu is the Cherokee term for snake, hence a snaky place. *Formerly called Mount Alexander, in honor of Princeton University professor Stephen Alexander.

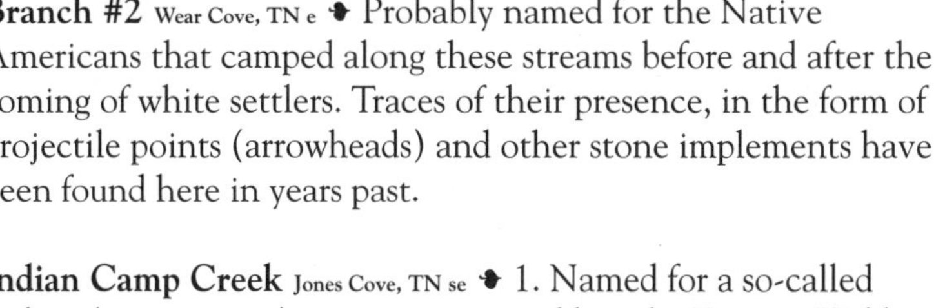

Indian Camp Branch #1 Mt. Le Conte, TN/NC w-m **Indian Camp Branch #2** Wear Cove, TN e ❧ Probably named for the Native Americans that camped along these streams before and after the coming of white settlers. Traces of their presence, in the form of projectile points (arrowheads) and other stone implements have been found here in years past.

Indian Camp Creek Jones Cove, TN se ❧ 1. Named for a so-called Indian (or primitive) camp constructed here by Tommy Webb, the younger brother of Eli Webb, the first settler in the Cosby area. 2. So named because it was a camping place for the Indians that once raided the settlers in this area. A number of Native American artifacts have been found along this stream.

Indian Cemetery Bryson City, NC n ❧ 1. Probably so-named because Native Americans are buried here. 2. Could be named for its proximity to Indian Creek.

Indian Flats Luftee Knob, NC/TN se ***n.l.*** **Indian Flats Falls** Thunderhead Mt., NC/TN ne ***n.s.*** **Indian Flats Prong** Thunderhead Mt., NC/TN ne-n ❧ Indian Flats is named for the former presence of a Cherokee camp in this area. As early as 1875 it was noted that the site had formerly been occupied by Indians as evidenced by an abandoned cultivated field, fire rings, broken stones, and pottery shards.

Indian Gap Clingmans Dome, NC/TN n ❧ So named because an ancient Indian trail between what is now North Carolina and Tennessee passed through this gap. It was widened in the 1830s to accommodate wagons and cattle. Another road through this gap was also constructed by Thomas' legion of Confederate Cherokee soldiers (see Thomas Divide) during the Civil War (1862) to provide access to Alum Cave, where mineral salts could be mined for use in making gun powder at a North Carolina arsenal. Previously called Road Gap, Old Road Gap, Luftee Gap, Smoky Gap, Wears Gap, Grassy Gap, Collins Gap, Walase (frog) gap, and probably other names.

Indian Grave Flats Clingmans Dome, NC/TN nw ❧ While raiding the area around Cherokee, North Carolina, during the Civil War, Federal troops took several Indians captive. As they retreated through Indian Gap, one brave was shot and left for dead. Confederate troops found him, and although they tried to nurse him back to health, he died. He is thought to be buried two miles below the gap, at Indian Grave Flats.

Steam engine on Injun Creek

Indian Head Rock Wear Cove, TN m *n.s.* ❧ Named for a cliff that resembles the profile of an Indian's head.

Injun Creek Mt. Le Conte, TN/NC ne-n-m ❧ Believed to be named for a steam engine that wrecked here in the 1920s and ended up in the creek. In this case, injun should probably be spelled "engine." Formerly called Indian Creek.

Ivy Branch* Cades Cove, TN/NC e **Ivy Gap** Cove Creek Gap, NC nw **Ivy Ridge** Cades Cove, TN/NC se ❧ Ivy is an old mountain term for mountain laurel (*Kalmia latifolia*) that, along with rhododendron, grows in profusion in these areas. *Formerly called Laurel Branch.

Jack Bradley Branch Clingmans Dome, NC/TN ne ❧ The Bradleys migrated from Rutherford County, North Carolina, to settle on the Oconaluftee River and its tributaries.

Jakes Creek, Jakes Gap Silers Bald, NC/TN nw ❧ 1. Named for Jake Houser who built a cabin and lived on this stream. 2. Named for

Jake Halman. 3. Named for Jake Cattern who lived with his wife on this stream. 4. Named for Jake Parton.

James Camp Branch Silers Bald, NC/TN w ❧ Probably named for a James family (possibly a William or Robert James) that once lived on or had a hunting or fishing camp along this stream.

James Gap Mt. Le Conte, TN/NC m **James Ridge** Mt. Le Conte, TN/NC ne-e-m ❧ Named for Dallas James (or perhaps his father) who lived near the Sevier County community of Rayfield, Tennessee.

Jay Bird Branch Gatlinburg, TN w ❧ Probably named for the blue jay (*Cyanocitta cristata*), a noisy, aggressive, and bright blue bird that is common in the park. Could be named for the fact that mountain boys went skinny-dipping in this stream and that the name could relate to the old expression, "naked as a jay bird."

Jesse Ridge Cove Creek Gap, NC sw ❧ Probably named for the Jesse Palmer family that had a small grist mill in this area. The Palmers lived in the area from the 1830s until park establishment.

Jim Mac Branch Smokemont, NC w-nw ❧ Probably named for Jim MacMahan, a former resident of this area. Formerly called Jim MacMahan Branch.

Jim Ute Branch, Jim Ute Ridge Clingmans Dome, NC/TN sw ❧ Probably named for Jim Ute Wiggins who lived at one end of this ridge. Ute was a shortened version of the biblical name Urijah, often used by mountain people.

John Henry Camp Creek Bunches Bald, NC s-m ❧ Probably named for the John Henry family and possibly the site of a former logging camp. John Henry could also be the first and middle names of a man or boy, surname unknown.

John Mack Creek Luftee Knob, NC/TN ne-e ❧ Probably named for M.B. (Johnny) MacMahan of Sevier County, Tennessee.

Joint Ridge Wear Cove, TN e-m ❧ Probably named for the fact that this is one of three joint (joined) ridges or spurs off Roundtop.

Jonas Creek Silers Bald, NC/TN m-s ❧ Probably named for Jonas Jenkins who once lived in this area.

Jump-off, The Mt. Le Conte, TN/NC se ❧ This is a quaint or picturesque name derived from the fact that if someone wanted to commit suicide, he or she could certainly do it by jumping off this shear 1,000 foot cliff.

Juney Whank Falls

Jumpup Ridge Noland Creek, NC nw-n ❧ 1. Could be related to an old mountain expression to jump up a mountain or hill, meaning to run up the hill and jump over obstacles while fleeing from an animal such as a bear. 2. Another reference defines jumpup as meaning steep, as in a steep ridge.

Juney Whank Branch, Juney Whank Falls Bryson City, NC n ❧ This stream and falls are probably named for Junaluska (Juney) Whank, who is said to be buried in this area. He was named for the famous Cherokee Chief, Junaluska. Juney Whank is thought to be Cherokee for "place where the bear passes."

Kahneska Branch Luftee Knob, NC/TN sw ❧ Named for the Cherokee term for grassy. See Grassy Branch.

Kalanu Prong Mt. Guyot, TN/NC w-sw ❥ Named for a Cherokee chief who lived in this area around the time of the American Revolution. It is also the Cherokee name for Sam Houston, or anyone named Houston. Formerly called Boat Gunnel Flats.

Kanati Fork Smokemont, NC nw-w ❥ 1. Named for the Cherokee term for lucky hunter. 2. Named for the legendary first man in Cherokee mythology. He was the Biblical equivalent of Adam who kept animals, like bears, penned up in a cave until they were needed for food. His wife was Selu and their sons were the Thunder Boys.

Katalsta Ridge Mt. Guyot, TN/NC s-se ❥ Named for the daughter of the great Cherokee chief Yonaguska (Drowning Bear). She was said to be a talented Cherokee pottery maker.

Kear Branch Mt. Le Conte, TN/NC nw ❥ Named for the family of an early Scotch settler in the Gatlinburg area. They arrived in Sevier County, Tennessee, in 1808 or 1809. Also see Carr Branch.

Keeyuga Creek Silers Bald, NC/TN se ❥ Named for the Cherokee term for chipmunk (*Tamias striatus*).

Keg Drive Branch Clingmans Dome, NC/TN m ❥ The favorite bear driving (hunting) spot for many, including Jim Keg, an Indian and a soldier in the Cherokee Company of the Thomas Legion (see Thomas Divide), formed in 1802. The term drive was associated with bear hunting since the dogs were expected to seek out the bears and drive them (hopefully) back toward the hunters.

Kelly Bennett Peak Bryson City, NC nw ❥ Named for Dr. Kelly E. Bennett (1890–1974), the so-called "Apostle of the Smokies," who was a close personal friend of Horace Kephart and no doubt inspired some of his writings about the area (see Mount Kephart). He was a pharmacist, former North Carolina senator and representative, Mayor of Bryson City for 14 years, and served on the City Council there for four years. He also represented Swain County on the North Carolina Parks, Parkway, and Forest Development Commission from 1949 until his death and served as its president from 1951– 1955. In this endeavor, he was just as committed as Kephart to preserving the Smokies for all time as a national park. He assisted Arno Cammerer (see Mount Cammerer) in determining the final boundary for the North Carolina side of the park in the mid 1920s. He was a very strong proponent of the park before and after its establishment. His wife was given the privilege of choosing this previously unnamed peak to be named in her husband's honor. It was a peak that she and Dr. Bennett faced from their front porch and often watched in the late afternoon.

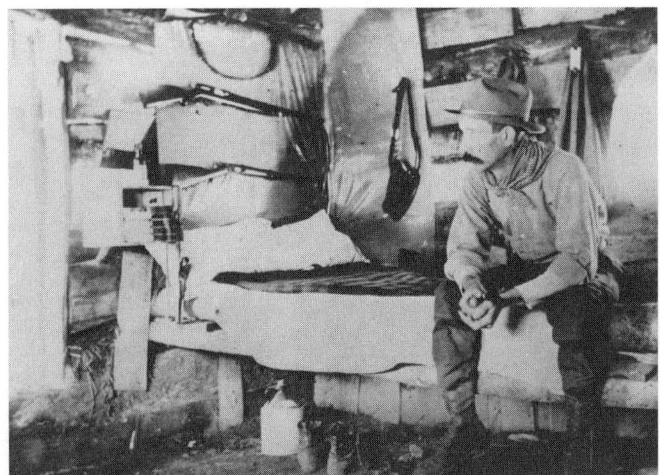

Horace Kephart

Kephart, Horace Memorial Clingmans Dome, NC/TN s ***n.l.*** **Kephart Prong** Smokemont, NC nw ❧ See Mount Kephart. The memorial was erected by the Kephart Troop of the Boy Scouts of America, Bryson City, North Carolina.

Killpecker Ridge Thunderhead Mt., NC/TN m ❧ This name probably refers to a rookie or new man on a logging crew, nicknamed a killpecker. This person was responsible for deciding which way a tree was to fall and/or chopping a wedge out of a tree trunk before the sawyers finished cutting it down with their crosscut saws. A naive new chopper (or pecker) might almost die of exhaustion before he learned to pace himself, cutting more accurately with fewer strokes. Hence, a killpecker.

Kingfisher Creek Blockhouse, TN se-s ❧ Named for a common bird of the Smoky Mountains, the Belted Kingfisher (*Ceryle alcyon*), which dives into the water for fish and other prey.

Kreider Branch Calderwood, TN/NC ne ❧ Probably named for a Krider (a slightly different spelling) family that once lived along this stream.

Kuwahi Branch Silers Bald, NC/TN e-ne ❧ Named for the Cherokee term for mulberry place, or just berrying place (no specific type of berry). See also Clingmans Dome.

Lands Creek Bryson City, NC w-nw ❧ Named for a Lands family that once lived in this area.

Laurel Branch #1 Gatlinburg, TN w-sw **Laurel Branch #2** Mt. Guyot, TN/NC w **Laurel Cove Creek** Thunderhead Mt., NC/TN nw **Laurel Creek #1** Cades Cove, TN/NC ne **Laurel Creek #2** Cove Creek Gap, NC nw **and other "laurel" place names** ❧ Named for the abundance of mountain laurel (*Kalmia latifolia*) within these areas. Also refers to rhododendron. Mountain people often referred to rhododendron as laurel and mountain laurel as ivy.

Laurel Falls

Laurel Top Mt. Guyot, TN/NC sw ❧ A local citizen, while standing on this peak, coined a sentence that gave it its name. "I'd rather be a knot on laurel (as in a topknot) than to live down at Smokemont." Formerly called Lover's View.

Law Branch Cades Cove, TN/NC nw ❧ Named for a Law family that settled on the west end of Cades Cove sometime prior to the Civil

War. A Henry Law still owned property on this stream when the land was purchased for establishment of the park.

Lawson Gant Lot Cades Cove, TN/NC m **Lawson Gant Lot Branch** Cades Cove, TN/NC e-se ❥ Named for a Daniel B. Lawson family that settled in Cades Cove around 1880. 1. Gant (a variation of gaunt) lots were fenced enclosures, high in the mountains, where cattle or sheep were corralled and kept off feed for a time prior to being driven down the mountain to market, slaughter, or winter pasture. Since these animals had spent the season eating green grass and getting fat and lazy, it was felt that they needed a rest period in which to get gant or nimble, before the long trek. 2. This name was also applied to an enclosure (a sort of gauntlet) where animals were separated by different owners, for the trip down the mountain. 3. The animals could grow very gaunt (gant) from a long wait in these lots if their owners did not immediately show up to herd them away. There were gant lots at Gregory Bald, Spence Field, Hannah Mountain and on a section of Mollies Ridge (the Dan Lawson range), and other locations.

Lazy Branch Dellwood, NC nw ***n.l.*** ❥ This picturesque name is probably just descriptive of the slow or easy course of this stream, as opposed to a stream like Roaring Fork that is fast and furious.

Leadbetter Ridge Cades Cove, TN/NC e-ne ❥ Named for a Leadbetter (actually spelled Ledbetter) family that settled on the east end of Cades Cove in the mid 1800s. Formerly called Mill Ridge.

Lead Cove Trail* Thunderhead Mt., NC/TN nw ***n.s.*** **Leading Ridge**** Cades Cove, TN/NC ne-n **Leadmine Ridge** Hartford, TN/NC s ❥ Named for deposits of lead ore (also called galena) in these areas. Locals often mined these deposits to make lead shot for their rifles as well as lead sinkers for fishing lines. *Formerly called Sandy Gap Trail. The present name relates back to the Civil War when lead mined in the Smokies was transported along what was then called the Lead Cove Road. **Formerly called Cave Ridge.

Leanto Branch Silers Bald, NC/TN m ***n.l.*** ❧ The name probably refers to a lean-to once built along this stream to provide shelter. Lean-tos are usually constructed of tree limbs and slabs of bark and have a single sloping roof structure.

Leatherwood Branch #1 Waterville, TN/NC sw **Leatherwood Branch #2*** Cove Creek Gap, NC nw ❧ Probably named for the Leatherwood families, pioneers in these areas. *Probably named for the John Leatherwood family that settled on Jonathan Creek, just south of the present park boundary, in the 1790s. They were the first family with this surname to settle in the area and they became prosperous.

Le Conte Creek Gatlinburg, TN e ❧ See Mount Le Conte. Once called Mill Creek, because there were 25 mills on this stream.

Ledge, The, Ledge Bald Luftee Knob, NC/TN s **Ledge Creek** Bunches Bald, NC n ❧ The Ledge is a narrow edge, or ledge, formation on the flank of Balsam Mountain. The bald and creek are in close proximity.

Lester Prong Mt. Le Conte, TN/NC se ❧ Probably named for Lester Shults-Ownby who once lived along this stream.

Lewellyn Branch Fontana Dam, NC n-m ❧ Probably named for a Lewelling or Luaalling family that once lived in this area.

Licklog Branch Cades Cove, TN/NC m-w **Licklog Gap** Tuskeegee, NC ne ❧ Deer, cattle, and other animals need mineral salts that they don't get from grazing or browsing. Deer satisfy this requirement from natural mineral salt licks. Domestic animals, like cattle, often must have it supplied to them by farmers. In the early days, Smoky Mountain herders would cut deep notches in downed trees, or find hollowed out

Licklog

logs, and place rock salt in them for their livestock. Undoubtedly there were once salt licklogs along this steam and at this gap.

Lindsey Creek Mt. Le Conte, TN/NC ne ✦ Named for a Lindsey family. Several Lindseys were living along this stream when the park was created. Jesse Lindsey received land grant #23839 in this area on June 19, 1841.

Line Springs Road Wear Cove, TN e ✦ Named for the old Line Springs Resort Hotel located north of the park boundary above Wear Cove. Also called Wear Cove Road.

Little Bottoms *n.l.*, Little Bottoms Trail* Calderwood, TN/NC ne ✦ Name derived from the choice, rich agricultural acreage (called bottom land) on either side of this section of Abrams Creek. This was once some of the best land in the area. See definition for term bottom. *Sometimes called Little Bottoms Manway, formed by a century and a half of use rather than by park trail builders. Once known as "the goat trail," because it was so narrow and treacherous in places.

Little Cataloochee Creek, Little Cataloochee Valley Cove Creek Gap, NC m-w ✦ See Cataloochee Divide. The Little Cataloochee Valley began to be populated when the (Big) Cataloochee Valley became overcrowded around 1899.

Little Duck Hawk Ridge Mt. Le Conte, TN/NC s ***n.l.*** ✦ Named for the Peregrine Falcons (*Falco peregrinus*) that have nested here. Called duck hawks by the old timers, these falcons kill birds (including ducks) in midair. They are one of the swiftest birds on earth. Widespread use of the pesticide DDT eliminated peregrines from the eastern United States, but they have since been reintroduced in many areas, including the Great Smoky Mountains. See Peregrine Rock.

Little Fork Thunderhead Mt., NC/TN sw ◆ In mountain vernacular, a fork usually describes a tributary of a stream. Little Fork is the site of the old Adams-Westfeldt Copper Mine.

Little Grill Ridge Cades Cove, TN/NC se-s ◆ Also known as Little Grille Ridge. See Big Grill Ridge.

Little Niagra Creek Mt. Guyot, TN/NC e-se ◆ This name may be a tongue-in-cheek comparison of this stream with the famous Niagra River on the Canadian/United States (New York) border.

Passenger pigeon

Little Pigeon River Mt. Le Conte, TN/NC n-ne ◆ Named for a once abundant and now extinct species of bird, the Passenger Pigeon (*Ectopistes migratorius*). The bird became extinct in Tennessee by 1893 and in North Carolina by the following year. Extinction was caused by overhunting.

Little River

Little River Silers Bald, NC/TN e-ne ◆ So named because, as rivers go, it is a relatively small one. However, it is one of the larger waterways in the park.

Little Tennessee River Noland Creek, NC w ◆ Named for this tributary of the main Tennessee River. Tennessee is believed to be a

Cherokee word, or a variation of one, whose meaning is lost in antiquity.

Loan Branch Wear Cove, TN s ❧ Possibly a map spelling error as the stream was formerly called Loon Branch for a Loon Grant Moore, who settled in this area with his wife Elizabeth. Ashley Branch, further downstream, is believed to have been named for their daughter.

Locust Cove Silers Bald, NC/TN s **Locust Gap*** Thunderhead Mt., NC/TN se **Locust Knob** Bunches Bald, NC m **Locust Ridge** Thunderhead Mt., NC/TN se-e ❧ Named for the presence of locust trees (*Robinia pseudocacia*), or more rarely (*Gleditsia triacanthos*), in these areas. *Formerly called Corner Tree Gap (see Balsam Corner).

Long Bunk Cove Creek Gap, NC w ❧ 1. Named for its resemblance (from a distance) to a bed or bunk. 2. During timbering operations, logs were loaded onto railroad flat cars in piles, or bunks as they were called by the loggers. Usually two bunks of 16 foot logs could be placed on a flat car. If the logs were longer than 16 foot, they were called long bunks. Those shorter than 16 foot were called short bunks and you might be able to get three bunks on a flat car.

Long Drive Ridge Clingmans Dome, NC/TN e ❧ 1. Name is probably related to long-distance cattle, sheep, hog, and turkey drives along or across this ridge in pre-park days. The animals were either being driven to market, slaughter, or from winter to summer or summer to winter pasture. 2. Name may also relate to hunting (see Keg Drive Branch).

Long Hungry Ridge Cades Cove, TN/NC sw ❧ Named for a site where a number of hunters were once marooned for several days due to a heavy snow storm. They constructed a make-shift shelter of downed trees and limbs and built a fire to wait out the storm. They exhausted what meager rations they had the first day or so and then had nothing to eat. By the time they arrived back in civilization, they had almost starved to death. Also formerly called Killpecker Ridge (see Killpecker Ridge).

Lookout Branch Silers Bald, NC/TN nw-n ❧ Probably named for Ben Parton Overlook to the northwest (see Ben Parton Overlook).

Lookout Rock Mt. Le Conte, TN/NC m ❧ A high point near Long Branch Gap where one can look out over a fine vista.

Loop, The Mt. Le Conte, TN/NC sw ❧ A point on the Newfound Gap Road (U.S. Highway 441) where the road curves to make a circle, going back over itself in a loop fashion. Prior to construction of this feature, the Newfound Gap Road was so steep at this point that some autos could not negotiate it.

Warning sign for The Loop

Lost Bottom Creek Luftee Knob, NC/TN s-se ❧ Named for the broad, flat bottom land along the middle section of this stream, in contrast with the upper and lower sections that are steep sided. This bottom land was probably cultivated in pre-park days, and would have been very secluded or lost to those outside of the valley. See glossary for term bottom.

Lost Branch Thunderhead Mt., NC/TN ne ❧ Name probably refers to the isolation or seclusion of this mountain stream.

Lost Creek Silers Bald, NC/TN ne ❧ Named for a creek that sinks or disappears beneath its rocky stream bed for some distance before resurfacing downstream.

Loudermilk Ridge Tuskeegee, NC ne-n ❧ Probably named for a Loudermilk family that once lived in this area.

Louis Camp Branch Smokemont, NC nw-n ❧ Named for a Cherokee Indian, Louie Owl, who had a camp on this stream and once hunted bears and other game here.

Lowes Creek Mt. Le Conte, TN/NC s-se-e ❧ Probably named for an early Sevier County, Tennessee, Lowe family.

Low Gap Luftee Knob, NC/TN n **Low Gap Branch** Luftee Knob, NC/TN n-ne ❧ Name refers to the relative low elevation of this gap, it being one of the lowest passes or trail crossings along the main crest of the Smokies.

Luftee Gap Clingmans Dome, NC/TN n **Luftee Knob*** Luftee Knob, NC/TN w ❧ This name is taken from the last two syllables of the Cherokee word Oconaluftee (see Oconaluftee River). Oconaluftee is a corruption of the Cherokee term Egwanulti that translates to "all towns along the river." *Also called the Pillar, or Pillar Head of Straight Fork of the Oconaluftee River. See glossary for term knob. At an elevation of 6,234 feet above sea level, this is the sixth highest free-standing peak in the park.

Lumber Ridge Wear Cove, TN s ❧ Name relates to pre-park timber industry in this area. Also see Mill Ridge.

Lynn Camp Branch Luftee Knob, NC/TN sw **Lynn Camp Prong*** Silers Bald, NC/TN nw **Lynn Camp Prong Cascades*** Thunderhead Mt., NC/TN ne ***n.s.*** ❧ 1. Named for a logging camp once operated here by Col. W. B. Townsend's Little River Lumber Company. Lynn is the loggers' nickname for the linden tree or American basswood (*Tilia americana*). 2. Name may also relate to a lin or linn that, in the vernacular of the Scotch-Irish, is a pool at the top or base of a waterfall. The many falls on Lynn Camp Prong would have many linns. *Formerly called Marks Cove Prong.

Lynn Creek Luftee Knob, NC/TN sw **Lynn Gap, Lynn Gap Branch** Calderwood, TN/NC se **Lynn Hollow** Blockhouse, TN se-s ❧ See Lynn Camp.

McCampbell Gap #1 Thunderhead Mt., NC/TN s ❧ Named for a McCampbell family that settled in this area prior to the coming of the park.

McCampbell Gap #2, McCampbell Knob* Cades Cove, TN/NC e ❧ Named in honor of an 1850s Cades Cove gold prospector, Robert (Bobby) McCampbell. *See definition for term knob.

McCaulley Branch Cades Cove, TN/NC n-ne-e ❧ Named for a James McCaulley family that settled in Cades Cove in 1897.

McClue Ridge Dellwood, NC w ❧ Probably named for a McClue family that once lived in the area. Could also be a variation of some other name, such as McClure.

McCracken Branch Clingmans Dome, NC/TN s ❧ Named for Joseph McCracken who settled on this branch with his wife Sarah Vaughn circa 1800. The site was previously known as McCracken Improvement (see Pierce Improvement).

McCully Branch Calderwood, TN/NC ne ❧ Named for a farmer who cultivated a large part of this area before park establishment. See also Andy McCully Branch.

McGee Branch Bunches Bald, NC nw *n.s.* **McGee Spring** Luftee Knob, NC/TN sw ❧ 1. May have been named for an Ira McGee family that had a farm near Round Bottom. 2. Named for a Rev. John McGee, a circuit riding preacher who probably never visited the area.

McKee Branch Dellwood, NC nw-n-w ❧ Named for a McKee family that settled in Haywood County, North Carolina, circa 1826. Has also been called McGee Branch which may be its proper name. Formerly called Long Branch and before that, a Cherokee name now lost in antiquity.

Madcap Branch #1 Bunches Bald, NC s **Madcap Branch #2** Smokemont, NC sw ❧ 1. This name is descriptive of the rushing, tumbling, and playful action of the water of these streams, especially during floods. 2. Named for a Madcap family. 3. Stream name is possibly a corruption of Metcalf (see Metcalf Bottoms) and may be named for a Metcalf family.

Maddron Bald* Mt. Guyot, TN/NC ne **Maddron Creek** Jones Cove, TN se ❧ Named for a Maddron family (probably Lawson and Annie Maddron) former residents of this area. *Formerly called Madders Bald, so possibly named for a Madder family. Could also have been named for bluets (*Houstonia serpyllifolia*), members of the Madder family of plants, which are common at this elevation and in open areas such as this bald.

Maggot Ridge, Maggot Spring *n.l.*, Maggot Spring Branch, Maggot Spring Gap Bunches Bald, NC e ❧ Supposedly named for small white worms often seen in the cold mountain springs in this area. These worms have been mistaken for maggots (fly larvae) and hence the name. The worms may be some species of planarian, small grayish flat worms.

Maloney Point Gatlinburg, TN m ❧ Named for General Frank Maloney (1879–1952), a Knoxvillian who served as president of the Great Smoky Mountains Conservation Association from August, 1944, until his death in March of 1952. Maloney was a military officer, planner, and civil engineer intimately familiar with the Smokies. In fact, he helped Arno Cammerer (see Mount Cammerer) establish the boundaries of the park. He surveyed and mapped the area to be acquired on the Tennessee side and provided other technical data. He also proposed the route of the Blue Ridge Parkway in North Carolina and conceived the idea of the Foothills Parkway in Tennessee. He later selected the route for the parkway, a 72-mile-long scenic highway, and shepherded the state and federal legislation necessary for its development. For this reason, he is known as the Father of the Foothills Parkway.

Manard Creek #1 Calderwood, TN/NC sw-s **Manard Creek #2** Cades Cove, TN/NC ne ❥ Probably named for a Blount County, Tennessee, Manard family that lived in this area before park establishment.

Manse Branch Luftee Knob, NC/TN sw ❥ Probably named for a manse in this area. A manse is a large house or mansion, usually a clergyman's home, particularly that of a Presbyterian minister.

Maple Sugar Gap Cades Cove, TN/NC e ❥ Named for maple sugar, which is made from the sap of sugar maple (*Acer saccharum*) trees.

Marks Creek* Thunderhead Mt., NC/TN ne **Marks Knob**** (Luftee Knob, NC/TN w ❥ Probably named for Mark Squires (see Mount Squires). *Marks Cove, through which this creek flows, was the site of an early lumber company camp. **At an elevation of 6,169 feet, it is the ninth highest free-standing peak in the park. Formerly called Cams Knob.

Martins Gap Clingmans Dome, NC/TN se ❥ Probably named for J. L. Martin, who once owned land in this area.

Marthas Branch Cades Cove, TN/NC n ❥ Named for the second daughter of John and Luraney Oliver. They settled in this area in the early 1800s.

Masa Knob Mt. Le Conte, TN/NC se ❥ Named for George Masa (1882–1931), an Asian-American photographer, artist, and scientist with a passion for geology. His Japanese name was Masahara Lisuka, but to his American friends he was simply George. He was a confidant and hiking companion of Horace Kephart (see Mount Kephart) and accompanied him and Charlie Conner (see Charlies Bunion) on a 1929 survey of intense storm damage along the Sawteeth Range of the Smokies. It was during this trip that Charlies Bunion, a familiar Appalachian Trail landmark, received its name. He was the first person to measure the length of many Smoky Mountain trails and the distances between prominent places using a bicycle contraption equipped with an odometer. He was a highly skilled outdoor photographer, and made many spectacular pictures of the Smokies. Many of these were used to promote the idea of preserving the area as a national park. He lived for four decades in the Asheville, North Carolina, area and loved the Southern mountains dearly. He was a charter member of the Carolina Mountain Club and helped establish the Appalachian Trail. (See glossary for term knob.)

Masonic Monument (or Shrine) Bunches Bald, NC s ❧ Constructed in 1937 with assistance of Masonic lodges throughout the United States using 677 rocks from around the world. The monument commemorates the benevolence of their organization.

Massie Gap Noland Creek, NC ne ❧ Probably named for a Massey (slightly different spelling) family that once lived in this area.

Mathews Branch Cove Creek Gap, NC sw ❧ Probably named for a Mathews (or Matthews) family that once lived along this stream.

Matt Branch, Matt Mountain Fontana Dam, NC ne-e ❧ Named for a Matt family that settled in the Hazel Creek area.

Meadow Gap Thunderhead Mt., NC/TN m ❧ Probably named for the fact that this gap was once a grassy area, devoid of trees, and either a remnant natural bald (see bald in glossary) or a cultivated area.

Meigs Creek, Meigs Falls* Wear Cove, TN s-se ***n.s.*** **Meigs Mountain** Wear Cove, TN se ❧ Named in honor of Return Jonathan Meigs, a surveyor who was commissioned to retrace the former (1797) Hawkins boundary line for an 1802 treaty with the Cherokee. His unusual first name came about as a result of the courtship of his father and mother. His mother was a Quaker who at first refused to marry her suitor. Each time he proposed, she refused. Trying one last time and being refused, he mounted his horse to ride away forever, only to hear his loved one say, "Return,

Jonathan, return." Thinking that "return" was the most beautiful word he had ever heard, he gave it to his son. * Formerly called Buttermilk Falls, Bridal Veil Falls, and Hidden Falls.

Meigs Post,* Meigs Post Prong Clingmans Dome, NC/TN nw ❧ A survey marker point established on August 17, 1802, on Mount Collins, showing the point at which the 1797 Hawkins survey line ended. Named for Return Jonathan Meigs (see Meigs Creek). *It is the point where a Cherokee Treaty line crossed the crest of the Smokies.

Meigs Post, 1926

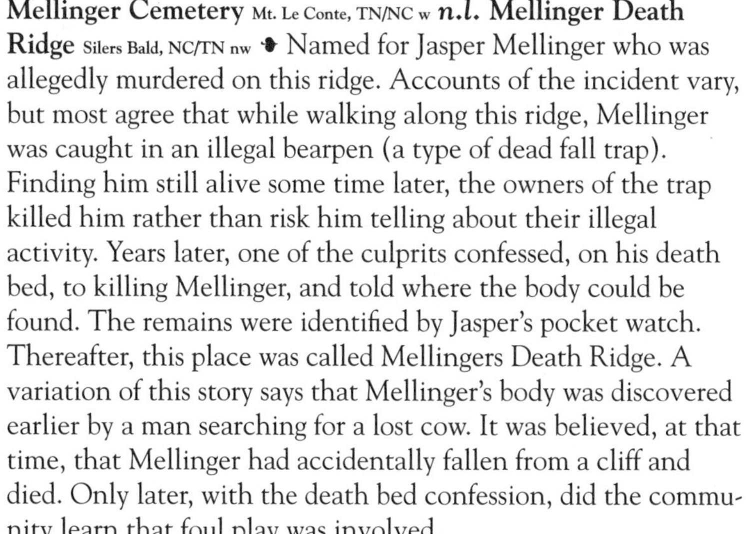

Mellinger Cemetery Mt. Le Conte, TN/NC w *n.l.* **Mellinger Death Ridge** Silers Bald, NC/TN nw ❧ Named for Jasper Mellinger who was allegedly murdered on this ridge. Accounts of the incident vary, but most agree that while walking along this ridge, Mellinger was caught in an illegal bearpen (a type of dead fall trap). Finding him still alive some time later, the owners of the trap killed him rather than risk him telling about their illegal activity. Years later, one of the culprits confessed, on his death bed, to killing Mellinger, and told where the body could be found. The remains were identified by Jasper's pocket watch. Thereafter, this place was called Mellingers Death Ridge. A variation of this story says that Mellinger's body was discovered earlier by a man searching for a lost cow. It was believed, at that time, that Mellinger had accidentally fallen from a cliff and died. Only later, with the death bed confession, did the community learn that foul play was involved.

Messer apple barn

Messer Farm* Cove Creek Gap, NC sw *n.l.* **Messer Fork**** Bunches Bald, NC ne ❧ *Named for the Christian Sargent Messer family that settled in Haywood County, North Carolina, in the 1780s. **Named for the Will Messer family that settled in the Smokies in 1895. Their apple barn is on display at the Mountain Farm Museum next to Oconaluftee Visitor Center. Formerly called Sugar Fork.

Metcalf Bottoms Wear Cove, TN e ❧ Named for Ridley and William Metcalf, two Cherokee Indians who came from North Carolina to settle in this area in the late 1800s.

Midnight Hole Falls Cove Creek Gap, NC ne *n.s.* ❧ So named because the plunge pool at the base of this waterfall is as dark as midnight, especially in the summer when green vegetation shades the area.

Mids Branch Gatlinburg, TN s-sw **Mids Gap** Gatlinburg, TN s ❧ Named for Middleton Whaley who owned land in this area prior to park establishment. His nickname was Mid.

Mill Branch #1 Calderwood, TN/NC ne **Mill Branch #2** Calderwood, TN/NC n-m **Mill Branch #3** Thunderhead Mt., NC/TN s **Mill Branch #4** Tuskeegee, NC m-n **Mill Creek #1** Cades Cove, TN/NC e-m-nw **Mill Creek #2** Calderwood, TN/NC w **Mill Creek #3** Clingmans Dome, NC/TN sw ❧ There were once many mill creeks, branches, and other streams in the Smokies, but the names of most have been changed. The name describes the former presence of grist, tub, gunpowder, saw, or some other types of water powered mills on these streams.

Cable Mill on Mill Creek (#1)

Mill Ridge Wear Cove, TN s ❧ Named for either a logging mill or a grist mill. William Marion Walker, who once lived at the base of this ridge, was a miller who also shaped and sharpened his own mill stones. However, nearby Lumber Ridge also attests to early logging operations in this area.

Millsap Branch Gatlinburg, TN sw-w ❧ Named for the Abram Millsap family that once received a Revolutionary War land grant of 2,000 acres in this area.

Mine Branch Clingmans Dome, NC/TN n ❧ Named for mineral explorations (prospecting and core drillings) that took place here around 1905.

Mine Mountain Bryson City, NC w-nw ❧ Probably named for an early local mine or prospect pits on this mountain.

Mineral Gap, Mineral Gap Branch, Mineral Gap Prong Thunderhead Mt., NC/TN m *n.l.* ❧ This name is related to the so-called Calhoun Digs. A man by the name of Granville Calhoun had a mining operation at this locale, just beneath Brier Knob.

Mingus Mill

Mingus Creek* Smokemont, NC sw-s **Mingus Lead** Clingmans Dome, NC/TN nw-n ❧ See Mount Mingus. *Formerly called Spillcorn Creek, for Jim Spillcorn who received a land grant here in 1805.

Mingus Mill Smokemont, NC s *n.s.* ❧ Named for the Mingus family, whose patriarch, John Jacob Mingus, settled along this stream in the 1790s. His grandson had the present turbine mill constructed by millwright Sion Thomas Early (or Earley) in 1886. It replaced an earlier overshot mill, constructed at the same site in the 1790s. The structure was renovated by the National Park Service in 1937 and again in 1968.

Mink Branch Calderwood, TN/NC e ❧ Named for a valuable furbearing mammal, the mink (*Mustela vison*), that is rarely observed but found throughout the park.

Minni Ball Branch Clingmans Dome, NC/TN ne ❧ Spelled differently, but named for a rifle bullet (a minié ball) used during the era of the

American Civil War. The name can probably be attributed to someone finding a minié ball along this stream, since there was Civil War activity in the area.

Miry Ridge Silers Bald, NC/TN nw-n ❧ Named for the presence of wet, sticky humus or black muck (rotting organic vegetation called mire), found within a hard rock basin formation along the top of this ridge. It is knee-deep in places, depending on the location and weather.

Moccasin Branch Clingmans Dome, NC/TN nw ❧ Named for a Native American shoe, the moccasin. Could have been named specifically for moccasin tracts found along this stream, or in theme with other nearby Indian place names such as Tomahawk Prong, Indian Grave Flats, and Indian Gap.

Mollies Butt,* Mollies Ridge, Mollies Ridge Spring Cades Cove, TN/NC m ❧ 1. Legend has it that this ridge was named for a Cherokee woman, Mollie, who died here searching for her lover White Eagle when he failed to return from a hunting trip. Her spirit is said to still haunt the ridge, and it can be seen in the night and early morning mists. 2. A molly or molly hogan is also a single strand out of a large logging cable. *See glossary for term butt.

Monteith Ridge Silers Bald, NC/TN n-m ❧ Named for the Monteiths, one of the first white families to settle in Swain County, North Carolina. They also settled in the Forney Ridge/Forney Creek area in the early 1800s.

Moore Springs, Moore Springs Branch Cades Cove, TN/NC sw ❧ Named for a Rev. Frank E. Moore, a Presbyterian minister from Maryville, Tennessee, who once had a cabin constructed along this stream.

More Liquor Branch Cades Cove, TN/NC nw ❧ This colorful name is suggestive of early moonshining activity in this area.

Morton Overlook Clingmans Dome, NC/TN n ❧ Named for Benjamin Andrew Morton (1875–1952), educator, merchant, manufacturer, civic leader, and president of H. T. Hackney Grocery (wholesale) Company. He served as mayor of Knoxville (1923–1927) and was a member, vice chairman, and finally chairman (from March 1952 until his death) of the Great Smoky Mountains Conservation Association. He was personally instrumental in acquiring the Champion Fiber Company tract, one of the largest and most strategic property acquisitions in the park.

Mount Ambler Clingmans Dome, NC/TN ne ❧ Named for Dr. Chase P. Ambler (1865–1932), an Ohio physician who moved to Asheville, North Carolina, in 1889 after reading an article in the Journal of the American Medical Association about the Great Smoky Mountains (and the area's health benefits). He was one of the pioneers in the movement to establish a national park in the Smokies and served as the first secretary-treasurer of the Southern Appalachian National Park Association in 1899. Although this organization brought the Smokies to the attention of the nation, it was unsuccessful in establishing a park. Ambler was also a primary supporter of the Weeks Act (which authorized U.S. Forest Service land acquisitions), and consequently the first tract of national forest land purchased under the Weeks Law (March 1, 1911) was dedicated in his honor.

Mount Buckley Silers Bald, NC/TN e ❧ Named for geologist and naturalist, Samuel Botsford Buckley (1809–1884). He was the first naturalist to describe the Smokies and its flora in some detail, including a couple of dozen new species and one new genus, *Buckleya*. He wrote in amazement about the flora of the Southern Mountains, especially the Smokies. He, along with other scientists such as Arnold Guyot (see Mount Guyot), made barometric pressure measurements of Southern peaks in the mid 1800s in order to calculate their elevations. It was, in fact, Guyot who named this peak in Buckley's honor. Measuring the heights of mountains was a rather inexact science in Buckley's day and his measurements were not always as accurate as those made by some other geographers. In fact, a number of the peaks he measured and named could not be identified years later from his manuscripts. Formerly called Buckley Peak. Elevation 6,582 feet.

Mt. Cammerer fire tower

Mount Cammerer Hartford, TN/NC se ❧ Named for Arno B. Cammerer (1883–1941), a native Nebraskan who joined the National Park Service in its infancy. He eventually became the director of the organization (1933–1940) and was a strong advocate for the development of a park in the Smokies. Cammerer was assigned the task of determining the final boundary for the park in 1924. He explored the area, with the assistance of such prominent men as Frank Maloney (see Maloney Overlook), Kelly Bennett (see Kelly Bennett Peak), and Horace Kephart (see Mount Kephart). He urged early acquisition of park lands before the lumber companies could strip them of all their virgin timber and before speculation caused prices to soar. In 1928, as associate director of the National Park Service, he convinced his good friend, John D. Rockefeller, Jr., to match state and local funding for purchase of the park. In fact, Rockefeller donated over five million dollars through the Laura Spelman Rockefeller Foundation. Formerly known as Bald Rock, White Rock, Sharp Top, and Old Mother (also see Chestnut Branch). Only one other fire tower in the eastern United States is designed like this one.

Mount Chapman Mt. Guyot, TN/NC e ❧ Named in honor of Col. David Chapman (1876–1938), owner of Knoxville's Chapman Wholesale Drug Company, and often called the father of the Great Smoky Mountains National Park. When first approached by fellow Knoxvillian Willis P. Davis and his wife (see Mount Davis) about working to establish a park in the Smokies, Chapman was not particularly excited about the idea. As a youth, he had hiked, hunted, fished, and camped in the Smokies and although he loved the area, he did not see it, at the time, as particularly significant or unique. However, after reading a 1902 report, drafted by then Agriculture Department Secretary James Wilson to President Theodore Roosevelt, expounding the natural beauty and uniqueness of the Smokies, he changed his mind. He not only became active in the movement, but became its greatest mover and shaker. Little did he realize the battle that lay ahead as he lead the effort to unite the states of Tennessee and North Carolina. Until that time, each state had a separate agenda toward the same goal. He helped raise the millions of dollars to purchase the property, convinced the Tennessee Legislature to use its powers of condemnation to acquire the land, and persuaded the U.S. government to establish the park. He gave not only his time and energy, but much of his own money to the cause.

Colonel David Chapman

In 1924, Chapman and others called on members of the Southern Appalachian Park Commission who were meeting in Asheville, North Carolina. This group was, at the time, inspecting potential sites for a national park in the eastern United States and the Smokies were not even on their list. Chapman was one of the Tennessee representatives who helped to remedy this. As a result the Smokies not only made the list, but became a top contender. Chapman was chairman of the Great Smoky Mountains Conservation Association from August 1931 until his death in 1944. He was also the first chairman of the Smoky Mountains Park Commission, established by the Tennessee Legislature in 1927. Chapman, more than any other individual, is credited with bringing the dream of a national park in the Smokies to fruition, and he diligently pursued the goal, even under the threat of his life from local anti-park residents and lumber company interests.

For these efforts, this mountain and U.S. Highway 441 from Knoxville to Sevierville were named in his honor. This peak was formerly named Mount Alexander by Samuel Buckley (see Mount Buckley), Old Black, and The Black. Also formerly called "Lumadaha." This name was created by using the first two letters of the names of four men, Lucine, Marshall, David (Chapman), and Harvey (Broome), and for a time was jokingly passed off as an Indian name. Its elevation is 6,417 ft. above sea level and it is the fourth highest free-standing peak in the park.

Mount Clark Smokemont, NC m ❧ Named for Admiral Joseph James (Jocko) Clark (1893–1971), a career naval officer and member of the western band of the Cherokees. A graduate of the United States Naval Academy, he was the highest ranking officer of Native American heritage in the U.S. military. He was a naval aviator in World War II and rose to the position of Admiral. He once commanded the aircraft carrier Yorktown, the famous "fighting lady" which probably wreaked more havoc on the enemy than any other sea-going ship in the history of naval warfare. During World War II he commanded Carrier Division 13 and during the Korean Conflict he lead the Seventh Fleet. He is alleged to be the grandson of General Stand Watie (see Mount Stand Watie).

Mount Collins* Clingmans Dome, NC/TN nw-w **Mount Collins Spring** Clingmans Dome, NC/TN nw ❧ Named for Robert Collins (1806–1863), one of the first settlers in the Oconaluftee Valley. He was the toll keeper on the Oconaluftee Turnpike, North Carolina, and a well-known Smoky Mountain guide. He guided Arnold Guyot (see Mount Guyot) and assisted him in determining the elevations of many of the high peaks in the Smokies in 1859. *At an elevation of 6,188 feet, it is the eighth highest free-standing peak in the park. Once called Mount Kephart by locals.

Mount Davis Thunderhead Mt., NC/TN e ❧ Named in honor of Willis Perkins Davis, a successful real estate agent and former manager of the Knoxville Iron Company. Davis and his wife Ann (see Davis Ridge) visited a number of national parks in the West in 1924 and returned with a dream of developing a park in the

Smokies. He shared this enthusiasm with a number of prominent Knoxville friends, among them Col. David Chapman (see Mount Chapman). Traveling to Washington, he presented the idea of a park in the Smokies to Dr. Herbert Work, then Secretary of the Department of the Interior, and found him very receptive to the idea. He became the first chairman of the Great Smoky Mountains Conservation Association in December of 1923 and served in this capacity until his death in August of 1931. Previously called Cold Springs Knob, Brier Knob, and Greenbrier Knob.

Mount Glory Silers Bald, NC/TN sw **Mount Glory Ridge** Silers Bald, NC/TN sw-s ❧ Said to be a glory because of the ease with which one can walk along the ridge. It is not too steep and its vegetation is not too thick. Formerly called Siler Knob.

Mount Guyot* Mt. Guyot, TN/NC e-ne **Mount Guyot Spring #1** Mt. Guyot, TN/NC e **Mount Guyot Spring #2** Mt. Guyot, TN/NC ne ❧ Named for Arnold Henry Guyot (1807–1884), a mineralogist, geologist, geographer, and a native of Naufchatel, Switzerland, who with financial support from the Smithsonian Institution conducted extensive research on the southern Appalachians between 1856 and 1860. Former head of the Geology and Physical Geography Department at Princeton University, he explored and measured the peaks along the state line ridge or crest of the Smokies and furnished the first accurate and detailed maps of the area. Even by today's standards, the elevations he calculated were surprisingly accurate—seldom being 20 feet different from present-day figures.

Survey tower on Mt. Guyot

Guyot was associated with such men as General Thomas Clingman (see Clingmans Dome), S. B. Buckley (see Mount Buckley), and Robert Collins (see Mount Collins) who helped map and determine the elevations of the Southern mountains.

He was responsible for naming many prominent Smoky Mountain peaks and other features including Clingmans Dome, Mount Love, Newfound Gap, the Sawteeth, and Tricorner Knob. His namesake peak was named by Samuel Buckley, a friend and colleague of Guyot. *Formerly called Balsam Cone and Balsam Pine. Known to the Cherokee people as *Sornook*, which may have been short for Osley Bird Saunook, a prominent Cherokee Chief. At an elevation of 6,621 feet, this is the second highest peak in the park.

Mount Hardison Luftee Knob, NC/TN w ❧ Named in honor of James Archibald Hardison (1867–1930), a Waynesboro, North Carolina businessman and politician, who served on the North Carolina State Park Commission and worked hard to promote the establishment of a park in the Smokies. At an elevation of 6,134 feet, it is the thirteenth highest free-standing peak in the park.

Mount Harrison Gatlinburg, TN m ❧ Thought to be named for Harrison Maples of the Elkmont area.

Mount Kephart Mt. Le Conte, TN/NC se ❧ Named in honor of Horace Soners Kephart (1862–1931), a writer, naturalist, and conservationist who greatly influenced the establishment of a national park in the Smokies. He was a world traveler, historian, Ivy League scholar, linguist, and librarian with the St. Louis Mercantile Library. Separated from his wife, children, and his job by alcoholism and finally a nervous breakdown, he moved to the mountains of western North Carolina in 1904. He came to the Southern mountains to get his life back on track and to pursue a literary career in a wilderness setting. He did much to bring the Smokies to the attention of the people and conservation associations across the U.S. through his writings. His most significant book was *Our Southern Highlanders* (1913), a classic study of the southern Appalachian people and their culture. His other writings included articles in *Field and Stream* and *Sports Afield* magazines as well as another classic book, *Camping and*

Woodcraft. This latter book and other articles led to him being called the "Dean of American Campers." He was obsessed with the natural and cultural environment of the Smokies and was particularly concerned over what he described as the increasing degradation of the area by timber companies. He was active in the establishment of the Appalachian Trail and even helped plot its route through the Smokies and North Georgia. The U.S. Geographic Board named this prominent peak in his honor in 1931, about two months before his death in a car accident in Bryson City, North Carolina. This was an unprecedented honor, previously reserved for individuals only after their deaths. At an elevation of 6,217 feet, it is the seventh highest free-standing peak in the park. Formerly called Pecks Peak, Mount Collins, Laurel Top, and Mount Alexander.

Mount Lanier Calderwood, TN/NC m-s ❧ Named for Sidney Lanier (1842–1881), the beloved Southern poet and musician whose grandfather, Sterling Lanier, owned and operated Montvale Springs Hotel. This resort was located just outside of the area that would eventually become the park and Sidney spent his summers here, hiking in the mountains and valleys. It was here that he wrote his only novel, *Tiger Lilies*, and it was here that he often played his flute to the delight of locals and tourists alike. His poetry demonstrated that he was a child of nature, an appreciation for which he surely gained in his beloved Smokies. He was most noted for his melodic poems, including *The Marshes of Glenn* and *Song of the Chattahoochee*. He served in the Confederacy during the Civil War where he contracted tuberculosis while a prisoner of war in Point Lookout, Maryland. He never recovered from the disease and died while convalescing in the mountains of North Carolina.

Mount Le Conte,* Mount Le Conte Spring Mt. Le Conte, TN/NC s ❧ Probably named for John Le Conte, a Georgia-born physician and professor of chemistry, physics, and natural history. John was the elder brother of Joseph Le Conte, for whom the mountain has traditionally (but erroneously) been thought to be named.

Mt. Le Conte

Joseph was a prominent geologist, Confederate Army chemist, and a contemporary of Arnold Guyot (see Mount Guyot). The mountain was named by Samuel Buckley (see Mount Buckley) in appreciation for John Le Conte's assistance in determining its elevation in the 1850s. John was one of the persons who took barometer readings at lower elevations at exactly the same time that Buckley was taking the readings on top of the mountain. The difference between these readings was used to calculate the elevation of the peak. *Unlike the surrounding mountains, Le Conte rises a mile from its base, making it perhaps the most impressive single mountain in the southern Appalachians. It is the third highest peak in the park, elevation 6,593 feet. Its Cherokee name was *Walasiyi*, the home of the giant mystical green frog (see also Buckeye Gap). Formerly called Central Peak and Smoky Mountain. Also formerly called Group of Bullhead, Tennessee. (See High Top, West Point, and Myrtle Point, which are all subpeaks of Mount Le Conte.)

Mount Love Clingmans Dome, NC/TN w ❧ Named in honor of Dr. Samuel Leonidas Love (1827–1887), who assisted Dr. B. S. Buckley (see Mount Buckley), and others in determining the elevation of Clingmans Dome, highest peak in the Smokies. Love was a prominent physician and political figure in Haywood County, North Carolina.

Mount Mingus Clingmans Dome, NC/TN nw-n ❧ Named for Dr. John Jacob Mingus, whose home and mill were built in this area. He was also one of the organizers of the Epsom Salts Manufacturing Company, which unsuccessfully attempted to extract and sell minerals from Alum Cave (see Alum Cave) in the 1830s. He settled in the Oconaluftee River Valley in the 1790s.

Mount Sequoyah Mt. Guyot, TN/NC e ❧ Named for Cherokee Chief Sequoyah or Sikwayi (1760–1843), a man of mixed white and Cherokee blood whose German ancestry name was George Gist. His father was Nathaniel Gist, a lieutenant colonel in Washington's Indian auxiliaries. His father abandoned him and his mother in the 1770s. His mother, Wureth, was a full-blooded member of the Cherokee Paint Clan and the sister of Chief Old Tassel. In his early adult years, Sequoyah was recognized as a good painter and silversmith. He later fought with Andrew Jackson's Tennessee Militia.

Chief Sequoyah

No other person in history is known to have invented an entire written language. He was never formerly educated, nor did he read or write English or any language other than Cherokee.

Mount Sequoyah was formerly known as the highest of three peaks, called "the Three Brothers," by Arnold Guyot (see Mount Guyot). At an elevation of 6,003 feet, this is the twelfth highest free-standing peak in the park.

Mount Squires Thunderhead Mt., NC/TN w ❧ Named for Senator Mark Squires (1878–1938) of Lenoir, North Carolina. As chairman of the North Carolina Park Commission, he lead his state's movement to establish a park in the Smokies during its early and most critical period. When many North Carolinians sought a national park in the Grandfather Mountain–Linville Gorge area, Squires opted for the Smokies location and a cooperative effort with Tennesseans. He worked closely with Col. David Chapman (on the Tennessee side) and others in establishing the park. He introduced a bill in the State Legislature in 1927 to establish a North Carolina Park Commission and an appropriation of $2 million to purchase property for the park. This bill challenged the state of Tennessee to do likewise. He became the first chairman of this 11 member park commission and later a member of the board of trustees that accepted and handled a five million plus dollar matching Rockefeller Memorial fund. Formerly called Little Bald.

Mount Stand Watie Smokemont, NC sw-s ❥ Named for Brig. General Stand Watie (1806–1871), a member of the eastern Band of the Cherokee and a Confederate army officer. Watie received his commission directly from Confederate States President Jefferson Davis. He was born in Rome, Georgia, the son of David and Susannah Oowatie. They called him Da-gata-ga, a name which means "stands firmly," and which was later anglicized to Stand Watie. A slave owner, he was a successful planter before and after the Civil War and a controversial figure with his people. He helped enact the Treaty of New Echota, ceding Indian lands in Georgia to the U.S. Government. Many Cherokees felt this an act of treason for their people. Eventually most of the Cherokees were repatriated west to reservations in the Oklahoma Territory, many along the infamous Trail of Tears in 1838. A raider and cavalry leader, he organized a strong group of Confederate Indians known as the "Cherokee Mounted Rifles." He was also the only Native American ever to reach the rank of general in the Confederate army, and he is believed to be the last Civil War officer to surrender to the Union in June of 1865. He is alleged to be the grandfather of Admiral Joseph James Clark (see Mount Clark). This mountain has also been called Watie Peak.

Mount Sterling* Cove Creek Gap, NC w **Mount Sterling Creek** Cove Creek Gap, NC w-nw-n **Mount Sterling Gap** Cove Creek Gap, NC w **Mount Sterling Ridge** Cove Creek Gap, NC w-nw ❧ 1. Named for the presence of lead around the Mount Sterling Creek bed, which, when first discovered, was thought to be silver. 2. Named for a logger from Sterling, Kentucky. *Formerly known by the names Devils Bedchamber and Old Field Balsam.

Mount Weaver Clingmans Dome, NC/TN n ***n.s.*** ❧ Named for Zebulon Weaver (1872–1948), an educator, attorney, and North Carolina Congressman and Senator for 28 years. His efforts to establish a national park in the Smokies began with the introduction of enabling legislation in 1923. This bill was co-sponsored by Kenneth McKellar of Tennessee. The measure finally passed in 1925. He also introduced legislation asking Congress to appropriate emergency funds to complete purchase of park lands in 1933 when the states of Tennessee and North Carolina were unable to raise the money necessary to match the Rockefeller Memorial funds. He was instrumental in the establishment of the Newfound Gap Highway, many miles of hiking and horseback riding trails in the park, as well as establishment of the Blue Ridge Parkway.

Mount Winnesoka Mt. Le Conte, TN/NC m ❧ Winnesoka is a Cherokee term meaning abundance of grapes, or place of the grapes. The peak is named for the wild grapevines found there.

Mount Yonaguska Luftee Knob, NC/TN w ❧ Named for Cherokee Chief Yonaguska or Ya'nu-gun'ski (1759?–1839), which means Drowning Bear. Previously called Ravens Knob by Arnold Guyot. Elevation 6,159 feet.

Mule Gap Silers Bald, NC/TN m ❧ Named for a mule lot (a fenced enclosure) at this gap owned by a Tom Siler. Also once known locally as Mule Lot Gap.

Murray Branch Calderwood, TN/NC w ❧ Probably named for the Cades Cove Murrays, some of whom received a 5,000-acre land grant there in 1838.

Muster Ground Cove Creek Gap, NC s ***n.s.*** ❧ Muster means to gather or assemble. This is a broad, flat area along the Cataloochee Road where locals once held community picnics, election campaigns, and where soldiers would make temporary camps.

Myers Branch Fontana Dam, NC e-ne ❧ Probably named for a Myers family that settled in this area. Some of the Myers still owned land here when the Tennessee Valley Authority acquired property for development of the Fontana Lake project.

Myrtle Point Mt. Le Conte, TN/NC s ❧ Named for a thick cover of Allegheny sand myrtle (*Leiophyllum buxifolium)* that once covered this rocky promontory. Heavy use of this area has destroyed much of this original brushy evergreen ground cover. Formerly called Murtle Point and North Peak. This has long been a favorite place for backpackers and Le Conte Lodge guests to watch the sunrise. Also called Mount Safford by Prof. S.B. Buckley (see Mount Buckley) when he explored and mapped these mountains in 1858.

Sand myrtle

Narrows Branch Silers Bald, NC/TN n-m **Narrows, The** Silers Bald, NC/TN m ❧ Named for a section of the state line ridge, along the Appalachian Trail, just east of Silers Bald. Here the ridge is knife-edged, (sometimes referred to as a hog back). See also The Sawteeth and glossary for hog back.

Negro Graveyard Cove Creek Gap, NC w ***n.s.*** ❧ Named for an African-American cemetery about which little is known. It is thought to have seven Negro slave graves and one white (stranger) grave.

Nellie*, Nellie Ridge Cove Creek Gap, NC sw ❧ Named for Nellie (Palmer) Wright, daughter of Turkey George Palmer (see Palmer Branch), who in 1907, at the age of one year, won first place in a baby contest. *The community of Nellie was established in 1848.

Nettle Branch Luftee Knob, NC/TN w-m-n **Nettle Creek** Clingmans Dome, NC/TN e-se **Nettle Creek Bald*** Clingmans Dome, NC/TN e ❧ 1. Thought to be named for the stinging nettle plant (family Urticaceae). 2. However, one of the early superintendents of the park was Harry L. Nettle, a native of North Carolina. *Formerly called Collins Creek Bald (see Mount Collins) and Kanati Bald (see Kanati Fork).

Newfound Gap Road, late 1920s

Newfound Gap Clingmans Dome, NC/TN n ❧ Named for a new, lower gap over the main range of the Smokies believed to have been discovered as early as the late 1850s (but one source believed that it was not discovered until much later). Prior to this, the only trans-mountain road over the range passed through Indian Gap about three-quarters of a mile west of the new gap. Formerly called Right Hand Gap and New Gap.

Newton Bald, Newton Branch Smokemont, NC w ❧ Named for a Newton family that once lived in this area. This was not a natural mountain bald, but was created by the Newtons, probably by deadening the trees on it. See glossary for terms bald and deadening.

Newt Prong Gatlinburg, TN sw ❧ Named for a species of salamander, the red-spotted newt (*Notophthalmus viridescens*) that inhabits this and other Smoky Mountain streams. The Smokies are noted for their wide variety of salamanders, with at least 30 species indigenous to the park.

New World Thunderhead Mt., NC/TN n ❧ 1. To escape from Civil War marauders, a group of Tennessee citizens left their homes and moved farther up into the mountains to seek solace and safety. Finding this beautiful and secluded cove, hidden from their old world, they called it New World. 2. John Walker once hiked up Thunderhead Prong so far that he saw nothing to indicate that anyone had ever been there before. That area was thereafter referred to as New World.

Nicks Nest Branch Clingmans Dome, NC/TN s ❧ Name refers to Old Nick, the Devil. See Devils Den.

Noland Creek, Noland Divide Bryson City, NC nw **Noland Gap, Noland Mountain** Cove Creek Gap, NC sw-s ❧ Named for William Noland, who moved into the Cataloochee area in 1839. He and his wife Elizabeth (Hannah) Noland were the valley's first permanent settlers.

Noyah Branch Silers Bald, NC/TN s-se ❧ Noyah is the Cherokee term for rock. This name refers to the rockiness of this stream.

Nuna Ridge Cades Cove, TN/NC se-e ❧ Nuna is the Cherokee term for potato. Formerly called Tater Ridge.

Nunda Branch Thunderhead Mt., NC/TN m-s ❥ Named for the Cherokee mythological term for sun or moon.

O

Oconaluftee River Smokemont, NC s-m-w-nw ❥ Oconaluftee is a corruption of the Cherokee term Egwanulti that translates to "all towns along the river." The original name of this stream was lost, so this word was adopted. It was referred to by white settlers in the 1790s as Newnai. Several North Carolina state grants also refer to it in the same way. Newnai was a white pronunciation of the word Nununyi, a Cherokee term for potato patch. Newnai was actually the name of a town on the Oconaluftee. Previously called Mingus Mill Creek. The section of the stream between Beech Flats Prong and Smokemont was previously called Luftee Prong.

Oconaluftee River

Ogle Hollow Blockhouse, TN se **Ogle Spring Branch** Jones Cove, TN se ❥ Named for the Ogle family (originally Oglesby), the first to settle at White Oak Flats (later Gatlinburg) in the early 1800s. They eventually spread throughout Sevier County and Blount County, Tennessee.

Ola Cove Creek Gap, NC w ❥ Named for the daughter of Will Messer. Will established a general store, blacksmith shop, and constructed other buildings in this area circa 1910. Most sources actually give her name as Viola, but some say Ola.

Old Black Mt. Guyot, TN/NC ne ❥ So named because this mountain appears dark from a distance due to its dense stands of conifer trees (red spruce and Fraser fir). Previously called Mount Henry by Arnold Guyot (see Mount Guyot). At an elevation of 6,370 feet, it is the fifth highest free-standing peak in the park.

Oliver Branch Cades Cove, TN/NC n ❧ Named for the Oliver family, early settlers in Cades Cove, and perhaps specifically for Tipton Oliver. His homestead is still preserved along this stream.

Tipton Oliver house

Oliver, John Cabin Cades Cove, TN/NC n ❧ Named for John Oliver, who, with his wife Lucretia and daughter Polly, are believed to have been some of the first non-Indian settlers in Cades Cove, circa 1818. This is one of the two oldest structures in Cades Cove (circa 1820s).

Oskodah Branch Luftee Knob, NC/TN nw-w ❧ This is the Cherokee term for buckeye, the nut of the buckeye tree (*Aesculus* sp.).

Otter Creek Mt. Guyot, TN/NC ne ❧ Named for the river otter (*Lutra canadensis*), a large weasel-like mammal once common along this and other park streams.

Overlook Ridge Bunches Bald, NC m ❧ A ridge overlooking (and providing a commanding panorama of) the surrounding area. Heintooga Overlook is on this ridge. Formerly called Trail Ridge.

Painter Branch Gatlinburg, TN e ❧ Painter is a local term for panther (mountain lion). See Panther Creek.

Palmer Branch Dellwood, NC nw-w **Palmer Creek** Cove Creek Gap, NC sw ❧ Named for a family of Cataloochee Valley settlers who entered the area in the 1830s and spread into the Little Cataloochee area in the 1850s. The original settlers were George Lafayette and his wife Nancy Jane. Two of the more colorful characters of this family were Turkey George Palmer and his son Robert (Boogerman) Palmer.

Turkey George Palmer

Panther Branch #1 Cades Cove, TN/NC e **Panther Branch #2** Hartford, TN/NC s **Panther Creek #1** Calderwood, TN/NC w-m-s-se-e **Panther Creek #2** Silers Bald, NC/TN nw **Panther Den Ridge** Thunderhead Mt., NC/TN se **Panther Gap** Cades Cove, TN/NC sw ❧ Panther is another name for mountain lion, also called painter, catamount, and catamountain. In the Western states, it is also referred to as a cougar or puma. Mountain lions were fairly common in the Great Smoky Mountains until hunting and trapping lead to their demise here.

Panther Spring Gap Dellwood, NC n ❧ Named for an incident where a young Jonathan Creek girl was allegedly dragged screaming through this gap by a panther in pioneer times. She was never seen again, and it was assumed that she was eaten by the large cat. This is a common folk tale theme in the U.S.

Pardon Branch Calderwood, TN/NC n ❧ Named for a Pardon (or Parton) family that once lived in this area.

Parson Bald, 1925

Parson Bald* Calderwood, TN/NC se **Parson Branch** Calderwood, TN/NC se-s **Parson Lead** Calderwood, TN/NC se **Parsons High Top** Calderwood, TN/NC se-e ❧ 1. Named for Joshua Parson, an early settler in the area who lived near the confluence of Abrams

Creek and the Little Tennessee River. He constructed the Parsons Turnpike along the Little River, circa 1829. 2. It may also have been named for religious revivals conducted here by ministers (or parsons) in the early 1800s. *Formerly called Great Bald.

Parton Branch Gatlinburg, TN m ❧ Named for a Parton family that settled in this area in the mid 1800s.

Paw Paw Creek Thunderhead Mt., NC/TN sw **Paw Paw Ridge*** Cades Cove, TN/NC se ❧ Named for the American pawpaw (*Asimina triloba*) a small tree with edible fruits.

Peawood Hollow Silers Bald, NC/TN ne ❧ Named for the silverbell tree (*Halesia carolina)* that is locally called peawood.

Peckerwood Branch, Peckerwood Ridge Calderwood, TN/NC e ❧ 1. May have been named for a small sawmill on this ridge or along this stream, since mountain people often referred to such operations as peckerwood or coffeepot mills. 2. Mountain folk also referred to woodpeckers (Picidae family) as peckerwoods, so it could have been named for the bird.

Pecks Branch Mt. Guyot, TN/NC s-m ***n.l.*** **Pecks Corner, Pecks Corner Branch, Pecks Corner Spring** Mt. Guyot, TN/NC s ❧ Named for a Peck family that acquired one of the first land grants in this area. The term corner refers to a marker tree, at the corner of two large state grants, issued May 29, 1838. One grant was awarded to Moses and Henry Peck and the other to Benjamin and Elliott Peck.

Peregrine Peak Mt. Le Conte, TN/NC s ❧ Named for the Peregrine Falcons (*Falco peregrinus*) that once nested here. Called duck hawks by the old timers, these falcons kill birds (including ducks) in midair. They are one of the swiftest birds on earth. Widespread use of the pesticide DDT eliminated Peregrines from the eastern United States, but they have since been reintroduced in many areas, including the Great Smoky Mountains. The peak resembles Italy's Leaning Tower of Pisa.

Peruvian Branch Richardson Cove, TN ne ❧ 1. Named for the Peruvian cherry, which is what the early loggers called mountain ash (*Sorbus americana*), a prevalent tree in the highest elevations of the park. 2. According to Horace Kephart (see Mount Kephart), this name was used by mountain people to refer to the pin cherry (*Prunus pensylvanica*). This is one of the only two non-Indian and non-American place names in the park. The other is El rado.

Phils View Gatlinburg, TN w ❧ This place is believed to have been named for Phil Hough, the park's first ranger. Interestingly, there is no view from this point.

Phoebe Branch Gatlinburg, TN s-se ❧ Named for the Eastern Phoebe (*Sayornis phoebe*), a bold bird that builds its nest of mud and moss under rock ledges, eaves, bridges, and tunnels.

Pickens Gap Thunderhead Mt., NC/TN sw ❧ Named for a Pickens family that settled in the Hazel Creek area in the late 1800s.

Pierce Branch Silers Bald, NC/TN nw-n ***n.l.*** **Pierce Improvement*** Silers Bald, NC/TN nw ***n.l.*** ❧ Pierce Improvement was a one-acre cultivated clearing named for a man called Pierce. It is said to have been cultivated each year from 1917 through at least 1927. The stream was also named for this man. *Improvement is a term once used to indicate the cultivation of land or construction of one or more structures on it.

Pig pen

Pig Pen Flats Cove Creek Gap, NC w ***n.s.*** ❧ Named for a hog enclosure (pig pen) once located along what is now the Long Bunk Trail. This trail was formerly called Pig Pen Trail for this reason.

Pilot Knob,* Pilot Gap Noland Creek, NC n **Pilot Ridge** Noland Creek, NC nw-n ❧ 1. So named because this knob, and possibly Pilot Ridge, were distinctive enough in profile and high enough in elevation to serve as landmarks or navigation points for the early travelers in this section of western North Carolina. 2. This knob (and area) was named for its sizeable population of pilot snakes, or copperheads (see Copperhead Branch). Legend has it that copperheads travel in front of rattlesnakes, guiding them, hence the name pilot snakes.

Pinkroot Branch, Pinkroot Ridge Cades Cove, TN/NC ne ❧ Pinkroot is a local name for the plant Indian pink (*Spigelia marilandica*). The wildflower is scarce in the Smokies, generally found only in the vicinity of Cades Cove.

Pinnacle Creek Cades Cove, TN/NC se **Pinnacle Lead** Mt. Guyot, TN/NC n-ne **Pinnacle Ridge** Fontana Dam, NC ne **Pinnacle, The** Tuskeegee, NC nw ❧ In the local vernacular, a pinnacle is a tall, sometimes slender, pointed formation, or an acute peak, ridge, or mountain.

Pin Oak Gap Luftee Knob, NC/TN s ❧ Named for a large oak once cut at this gap. Because the true pin oak tree (*Quercus palustris*) does not occur in the park, this name must relate to another species of oak, perhaps once called a pin oak by loggers or local residents. Since this was once called Spanish Gap or Spanish Oak Gap and the Spanish oak is a synonym for southern red oak (*Q. falcata*), the latter oak is the most likely candidate.

Place of a Thousand Drips Mt. Le Conte, TN/NC nw ***n.s.*** ❧ Named for an 80-foot high rock bluff above Roaring Fork where Cliff Branch spreads out to produce countless small falls and cascades that eventually join Roaring Fork along a 55-foot wide area. The falls varies from a trickle to a torrent depending on recent rainfall. Also has been called Spring of a Thousand Drips.

Poke Patch Backcountry Campsite Clingmans Dome, NC/TN m ❧ Named for the pokeweed plant (*Phytolacca americana*) that once grew in profusion around this campsite. Young, tender, pokeweed leaves were boiled by mountain people to make poke sallit, a nutritious, green, leafy food.

Pole Bridge Branch #1 Noland Creek, NC w **Pole Bridge Branch #2** Tapoco, NC/TN ne **Pole Knob Branch** Cades Cove, TN/NC e **Pole Road Creek** Clingmans Dome, NC/TN m-s ❧ 1. Possibly named for a corduroy road, constructed of poles or logs. Two or more long, parallel logs were laid down and others laid across them to form a raised road surface usually as a track for a piece of heavy equipment called a log hauler. 2. Possibly received its name from skid trails, built during the logging days, before park establishment. The skid trail was made by placement of perpendicular poles that logs could be slid down so as not to get hung up on rocks and other debris on the hillsides.

Polecat Branch Calderwood, TN/NC m **Polecat Ridge** Calderwood, TN/NC m-n-ne ❧ Polecat is a colloquial term for skunk. Two species live in the Smokies, the striped skunk (*Mephitis mephitis*) and the spotted skunk (*Spilogale putorius*).

Polls Gap Bunches Bald, NC e ❧ 1. Allegedly, Polly Moody's husband took their cows through this gap on the way to summer pasture. One year, he also took her favorite milk cow, which was pregnant at the time. As a result of the long and steep climb, the milk cow gave birth to her calf prematurely and both the cow and calf died. Polly threw such a tantrum over this loss that her neighbors named this gap Poll (short for Polly) in her honor. Formerly called Poles Gap. 2. Also called Pauls Gap by some old timers who insist that "it was named for an old man Paul."

Poplar Branch Gatlinburg, TN w **Poplar Cove** Luftee Knob, NC/TN ne **Poplar Flats** Noland Creek, NC nw **Poplar Hollow Branch** Smokemont, NC se **Poplar Pole Branch** Noland Creek, NC w ❧ Named for the presence of (tulip) poplar trees (*Liriodendron tulipifera*) in these areas. The tree is also called tuliptree and yellow poplar.

Porters Creek Mt. Guyot, TN/NC sw **Porters Creek Road** Mt. Le Conte, TN/NC e **Porters Flat** Mt. Le Conte, TN/NC e **Porters Gap*** Mt. Guyot, TN/NC sw **Porters Mountain** Mt. Guyot, TN/NC w-sw ❥ Named for James P. H. Porter, a prominent settler in Sevier County, Tennessee, who owned land and lived at Porters Flat (see glossary for term flat). *Formerly called Rhinehart Gap for a surveyor who carried a fellow surveyor, by the name of Ledbetter, on his back after Ledbetter became ill while surveying in the Smokies. Ledbetter died, but Rhinehart still had the gap named in his honor for the effort.

Dr. Calvin Post

Post Spring Cades Cove, TN/NC w ❥ Named for a Dr. Calvin Post (formerly a New York physician and early Smoky Mountain gold prospector) who acquired land on the southwest end of Cades Cove in the 1840s. See El rado.

Possum Hollow Tuskeegee, NC nw ❥ Named for the opossum (*Didelphis virginiana*), a common animal in the park and the only marsupial mammal (a relative of the koala bear and kangaroo) in the Americas.

Pounding mill

Pounding Mill Branch Wear Cove, TN e ❥ Named for a corn hammer, a water-powered mechanism constructed by Ben Stinnett, in 1897. It pounded or crushed (rather than ground) corn kernels into meal. The Cherokee used a similar method for making meal.

Powell Knob Cades Cove, TN/NC s **Powell Ridge** Cades Cove, TN/NC m-s ❥ Named for a George Powell family that settled in Cades Cove in the mid 1800s.

Proctor Tuskeegee, NC nw **Proctor Branch** Fontana Dam, NC nw-n **Proctor Creek** Silers Bald, NC/TN sw-w **Proctor Field Gap*** Fontana Dam, NC nw-n **Proctor Ridge** Silers Bald, NC/TN sw-w **Proctor Sang Branch**** Cades Cove, TN/NC s-se ❧ The town of Proctor was named for the Moses and Patience (Rustin) Proctor family that settled in the area circa 1830. The original home place was on the present site of Proctor Cemetery. William Proctor established a post office here in 1887. Upper Proctor was a segregated black community. The town of Proctor was abandoned with park establishment and isolated with the impoundment of Fontana Lake. *Named in honor of Jake Proctor, a resident of the area. **See also Seng Patch Branch.

Profit Branch Luftee Knob NC/TN ne ❧ Probably named for a Profitt (slightly different spelling) family that once lived along this stream. A Jackson Profitt was one of the earlier settlers in the Greenbrier Cove area.

Pullback Ridge Tuskeegee, NC n ❧ This name probably refers to descending this steep ridge, where one had to pull back on the reins to keep the horses, and/or wagon, from going too fast.

Puncheon Branch Wear Cove, TN e ❧ 1. A puncheon is a heavy, broad piece of roughly dressed timber, with one side hewed flat. Puncheons were once used to construct bridges and hence the possible origin of the name of this branch. 2. Named for long stakes (called puncheons) once driven into the ground to fortify Indian villages.

Making a puncheon

Purchase Gap Dellwood, NC n-m *n.l.* **Purchase Knob** Bunches Bald, NC m ❧ Revolutionary War Col. Robert Love purchased 5,000 acres of land which included the gap and knob. Once, while standing on the knob, he proclaimed "All the land you see is good land...but this is The Purchase," meaning Purchase Knob was the best of the land. The gap was named for the knob.

Queen Branch Bryson City, NC ne ❧ Named for a Queen family that once lived in this area.

Quillaree Branch Bunches Bald, NC nw ❧ Named for the Cherokee and early settlers' term for the Wood Thrush (*Hylocichla mustelina*), a small bird that produces an enchanting flute-like song.

Quill Rose Branch Cades Cove, TN/NC se ***n.l.*** ❧ Named for a colorful moonshiner, Quill or Aquilla Rose, who lived near the head of Eagle Creek and operated a mill and a blacksmith shop in the area.

Rainbow Cave Wear Cove, TN sw ***n.l.*** ❧ So named because a rainbow often forms in the entrance to this cave when the angle of the sun is right. The rainbow forms in the mist and spray of a small stream that tumbles over the cliff above the cave entrance. (Note: a permit is required to enter all park caves.)

Rainbow Falls Mt. Le Conte, TN/NC sw ❧ So named because a rainbow often forms in the mist and spray of this waterfall in the afternoon sun.

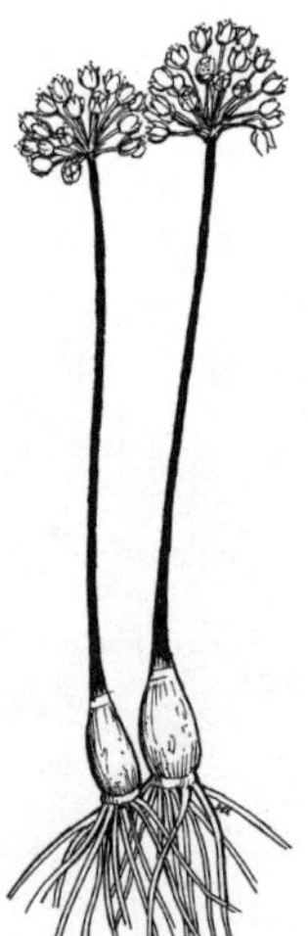

Ramp Cove Tuskeegee, NC nw **Ramp Cove Branch** Smokemont, NC ne **Ramp Creek** Gatlinburg, TN se ❧ Named for a type of wild leak or onion (*Allium tricoccum*) harvested in the spring by many mountain people. Ramps were often dug during the sign of Aries (March 21–April 20). The symbol for Aries is a ram, and for a time ramps were called "ram sons." Over time the name simply became ramps.

The plant is known for its strong taste and lasting odor. There is an annual Ramp Festival (a local celebration of the plant) at Cosby, Tennessee.

Ramsay Branch Mt. Guyot, TN/NC nw-w **Ramsay Cascades** Mt. Guyot, TN/NC n-m **Ramsay Prong** Mt. Guyot, TN/NC n-ne ❧ Named for the Ramsays, who settled in the Cosby area of what is now the national park in the mid 1800s.

Ramsey Creek Jones Cove, TN sw ❧ Named for a Ramsey family that once lived in the area. Spelling of family name could be a variation of Ramsay.

Rattlebox Branch Gatlinburg, TN sw-w ❧ 1. Named for a very noisy, steam-powered rock crusher (nicknamed the rattlebox) located on this stream. It furnished gravel for the construction of the Little River Road along the former route of the Little River Railroad line. 2. Named for a toy.

Rattler Branch Silers Bald, NC/TN ne-e ❧ Rattler is short for rattlesnake. See Rattlesnake Knob (following).

Rattlesnake Knob Clingmans Dome, NC/TN e **Rattlesnake Ridge** Silers Bald, NC/TN sw ❧ Named for one of the park's two poisonous reptiles, the timber rattlesnake (*Crotalus horridus*).

Raven Creek Mt. Guyot, TN/NC se **Raven Den, Raven Den Branch** Thunderhead Mt., NC/TN se *n.s.* **Raven Fork #2** Luftee Knob, NC/TN sw **Raven Ridge** Mt. Guyot, TN/NC e-se **Raven (Roost) Ridge** Bunches Bald, NC nw ❧ Named for the Common Raven, a majestic, jet black bird (*Corvus corax*) which spends most of its time at the higher elevations of the park. Ravens are the largest species of the crow family.

Raven Fork Overlook Smokemont, NC se **Raven Fork #1** Smokemont, NC se-s-ne ❧ 1. Named for Cherokee Chief Kalanu (the Raven) whose village was on this stream. In Cherokee, the stream was called Colehmayeh, from Coleh meaning raven and Mayeh meaning water. 2. Named for the large number of ravens (the birds) in this area (see Raven Creek).

Ravensford Smokemont, NC s-se **Ravensford Road** Smokemont, NC s ❧ Named for the Mingus family pioneer farmstead that probably took its name from Chief Kalanu (The Raven). See also Raven Fork #1 above. There was a shallow water crossing (ford) of Raven Fork #1 here.

Red Bird Branch Gatlinburg, TN w ❥ Named for the Northern Cardinal (*Cardinalis cardinalis*), a reddish bird with a crest (top knot) on its head. They are sometimes referred to simply as red birds. The cardinal gets its name from the scarlet colored robes of the cardinals of the Roman Catholic Church.

Red Man Creek (Left Fork), Red Man Creek* (Right Fork), Red Man Ridge Bunches Bald, NC w-m ❥ This name probably refers to Native Americans since it flows onto the Qualla Cherokee Indian Reservation. *Formerly called Indian Creek.

Red Oak Cove Luftee Knob, NC/TN n **Red Ridge** Fontana Dam, NC n-ne **Red Ridge Gap** Fontana Dam, NC n ❥ These areas were named for their abundance of red oak trees (*Quercus* sp.) and the brilliant red or scarlet color of their autumn foliage.

Redwine Creek Jones Cove, TN sw ❥ 1. Named for the James Redwine family (he was a circuit riding minister) who settled in this area. 2. Named for the abundance of wild grapes in this area.

Revenue Hill Calderwood, TN/NC s ❥ The name probably relates to former moonshine or whiskey making activities, the federal revenue tax not paid on it, or to early raids by revenue officers in this area.

Rhododendron Creek Mt. Le Conte, TN/NC ne-e-m ❥ Mountain folk often referred to mountain laurel (*Kalmia latifolia*) as rhododendron. Since there is more mountain laurel than rhododendron along this stream, it was probably actually named for the laurel.

Catawba rhododendron

Rich Branch* Silers Bald, NC/TN ne **Rich Butt Mountain** Hartford, TN/NC s **Richland Mountain** Smokemont, NC nw-w-n-m ❥ These areas were named for their rich, arable, or fertile soils. *This stream flows through Little Goshen, described in the Bible as fertile land (see Goshen Prong).

Rich Gap Cades Cove, TN/NC sw ❧ This gap served as a holding lot for cattle and other stock before their fall drive down to winter pasture, slaughter, or market. The presence of so much manure from these animals made the soil in the area very fertile (or rich). Formerly called Gant Lot (see Lawsons Gant Lot).

Rich Mountain* Kinzel Springs, TN se-s **Rich Mountain Gap** Kinzel Springs, TN s **Rich Mountain Road**** Cades Cove, TN/NC n ❧ *Formerly called Eldorado Mountain (see El rado). **Originally constructed in the 1830s. The present road was built by the State of Tennessee in the 1920s. Also once called Cades Cove Road.

Riding Fork Hartford, TN/NC s ❧ Probably named for James Riden, who purchased land here on December 10, 1880. Formerly called Ridens Creek and Caney Fork.

Ripshin Thicket Silers Bald, NC/TN m ***n.l.*** ❧ Probably so named because the rhododendron is so thick that it would rip your shins if you tried to travel through it.

Road Prong Clingmans Dome, NC/TN n-nw ❧ Named for the old Indian Gap Road, the Oconaluftee Turnpike (a toll road constructed during the Civil War) that once ran along this stream.

Road Turn Branch Gatlinburg, TN se ❧ Named for a very sharp turn in the old road, at this stream, before the present U.S. Highway 441 was constructed across the Smokies. Formerly called Lost Camp Branch.

Roaring Creek Thunderhead Mt., NC/TN m **Roaring Fork*** Mt. Le Conte, TN/NC s-m-w-nw ❧ So named because these are very swift and noisy streams. *This is one of the steepest (gradient) streams in the eastern United States. It drops a vertical distance of over 3,000 feet in five miles, and drops one mile in vertical distance from its headwaters to its mouth. It roars when it is high, someone once said, hence the name.

Rock Camp Branch Thunderhead Mt., NC/TN m ❧ Named for a rock shelter or overhang along this stream that loggers, anglers, and hunters used as a camp shelter.

Franklin D. Roosevelt at Rockefeller Memorial, 1940

Rockefeller Memorial Clingmans Dome, NC/TN n *n.s.* ❧ This huge rock monument, situated on the Tennessee-North Carolina state line, was erected in honor of Laura Spelman Rockefeller, mother of John D. Rockefeller, Jr. It commemorates the $5 million plus Rockefeller donation toward acquisition of the land for development of Great Smoky Mountains National Park. The year 1928 marked the lowest ebb in the park movement—land prices skyrocketed (based on speculation), efforts to solicit park acquisition funds from Henry Ford failed, and private donations dwindled. Fortunately, Rockefeller, who had given money for the acquisition and development of other national parks and monuments across the country, came to the rescue. He vowed to match, dollar for dollar, all money the states, local governments, and private citizens could raise to purchase the park. The park was dedicated by President Franklin D. Roosevelt from this monument September 2, 1940, before a crowd of 10,000 spectators. Rockefeller was not present for the dedication.

Rock House Cove Creek Gap, NC nw *n.s.* ❧ Name given to a 30-foot high cave-like formation in a boulder field, about 200 feet above Big Creek Trail. This rock shelter was inhabited by a number of early pioneers while they were constructing their permanent cabins along Big Creek.

Rocky Top Thunderhead Mt., NC/TN w ❧ Named for a rocky outcrop forming a small knoll on Thunderhead Mountain.

Roses Branch, Roses Gap Luftee Knob, NC/TN sw ❧ Named for Al Rose, a locating engineer with the Ravensford Lumber Company. He helped survey the route of the railroad spur that ran up through the Three Forks area of Hyatt Ridge.

Ross Knob Luftee Knob, NC/TN n ❧ Probably named for former park superintendent Blair A. Ross who served from 1945 to 1949.

Rough Arm Silers Bald, NC/TN w-sw **Rough Arm Branch** Silers Bald, NC/TN sw ❧ Many old timers used the term arm to refer to a ridge or a spur of a ridge or mountain. The "rough" could refer to the ruggedness of the terrain or a Rough family that was one of the original settlers on Mingus Creek in the Oconaluftee area.

Rough Creek* Clingmans Dome, NC/TN nw **Rough Fork**** Bunches Bald, NC ne **Rough Mountain** Luftee Knob, NC/TN n-ne ❧ *Previously called Ugly Fork. **Previously called Ugly Creek. The name could refer to the ruggedness of the terrain. There is also the possibility that "rough" could refer to a Rough family, since a Hosey Rough was one of the original settlers on Mingus Creek in the Oconaluftee area.

Rough-Hew Ridge Silers Bald, NC/TN s-se ❧ 1. Name may be related to early farming on this ridge, since hew, or to hew out, refers to the clearing of land. 2. Name may also refer to the old logging term, roughlock, which involved the use of a small dogwood log or pole placed between the spokes of both back wheels of a wagon when moving logs down hill. The front wheels would turn but the back wheels would skid, as a braking mechanism.

Round Bottom, Round Bottom Creek Bunches Bald, NC n-nw ❧ So named because this is a wide, flat, relatively round, bottom land valley. Once occupied by cultivated areas called the McGee fields, named for the settler who cleared them, Ira McGee.

Round Top* Mt. Le Conte, TN/NC m **Roundtop** Wear Cove, TN e **Roundtop Knob** Clingmans Dome, NC/TN w ❧ So named because the tops of these peaks are more or less rounded, domed, or conical in shape. *Once called Winnesoka (place of the grapes) by the Cherokee Indians.

Rowans Creek Cades Cove TN/NC ne-n-e ❧ So named because it was said to run by old man Rowan's house.

Rowdy Creek*, Rowdy Ridge** Hartford, TN/NC s ❧ 1. So named because these were favorite places for men and boys to gather for loud, roughneck, or rowdy parties. 2. Name is a picturesque description of a rushing mountain stream and its associated mountain. *Formerly called Leading Creek. **Formerly called Leadmine Ridge.

Russell Field, Russell Field Branch, Russell Field Spring Cades Cove, TN/NC e ❧ Named for a Russell Gregory family that lived on, farmed, and grazed stock on this high mountain bald in the 1800s.

Russell Hollow Wear Cove, TN m ❧ Named for John Russell who once lived in this area.

Rutile Branch Thunderhead Mt., NC/TN s-se ***n.l.*** ❧ Rutile is the mineral name for titanium dioxide, which is abundant in this area. It is a strong, low-density, highly corrosive-resistant, lustrous white metallic substance used commercially in the production of heat-resistant steel for aircraft and exceptionally white paint pigments.

Rye Patch, Rye Patch Branch Cades Cove, TN/NC sw ❧ Named for a broad section of Long Hungry Ridge where a Richard Russell planted rye grass just before the Civil War. The rye now grows beneath a mixed forest canopy.

Rye Patch

Sag Branch Dellwood, NC nw ❧ A sag is a low-lying area along a ridge or mountain top, not as pronounced as a gap.

Sahlee Creek Clingmans Dome, NC/TN n ❧ 1. This is the Anglicized name of a Cherokee leader who was executed by the U.S. government near Bryson City. The name is actually a variation of the Cherokee term Tsali. 2. The name could also be a corruption of the word shaley, for the shale rock found in the Smokies.

Salola Branch Clingmans Dome, NC/TN w ❧ Salola is derived from the name of a celebrated Cherokee metal worker Salali. The name is attributed to the 1940s Smoky Mountain Nomenclature Committee that was trying to find Indian names (or fabricate Indian-sounding words) that were short, musical, and easily pronounceable by English-speakers. Salali is also the Cherokee term for squirrel.

Sal Patch Gap Cove Creek Gap, NC s ❧ Named for Sally (Sal) Hannah, one of the earliest settlers in this area. The patch part of the name may refer to a garden patch.

Salt Branch Silers Bald, NC/TN w ***n.l.*** ❧ Name may be related to mineral salt deposits (natural salt licks) along this stream.

Sams Creek Thunderhead Mt., NC/TN e-ne-n **Sams Gap** Thunderhead Mt., NC/TN e **Sams Ridge** Thunderhead Mt., NC/TN m-n-ne ❧ 1. May have been named for Sam Cook, an early settler in this area. 2. May have been named for a Sams family that once lived in this area.

Sassafras Branch Clingmans Dome, NC/TN sw-s **Sassafras Gap** Fontana Dam, NC n **Sassafras Knob** Clingmans Dome, NC/TN s ❧ Named for the presence of sassafras trees (*Sassafras albidum*) at these locations.

Sawbrier Branch Thunderhead Mt., NC/TN se **Saw Brier Purgatory*** Clingmans Dome, NC/TN nw *n.s.* **Sawbrier Ridge** Thunderhead Mt., NC/TN se ❧ Sawbrier is a nickname for greenbrier (*Smilax* sp.), a heavily-thorned woody vine. *Refers to a very steep, rocky, and rugged area having a particularly heavy growth of greenbrier (see also Devil Branch).

Sawdust Pile Backcountry Campsite Tuskeegee, NC n *n.s.* ❧ Named for a large mound of sawdust generated by a small, private sawmill that operated here before park establishment.

The Sawteeth

Sawteeth, The Mt. Guyot, TN/NC sw ❧ This name describes a section of the crest of the Smokies where exposed, steeply-tilted, severely-weathered bedrock forms a jagged ridge. This sharp ridge crest resembles the teeth of a giant saw. This Sawteeth formation ranges from three feet to mere inches in width in places. This is a classic example of a hog back ridge (see glossary for term hog back). The Appalachian Trail runs along the Sawteeth, and here the hiker is literally walking with one foot in Tennessee and the other in North Carolina.

Scarlet Ridge, Scarlet Ridge Creek Silers Bald, NC/TN sw-s ❧ Probably named for the red oaks, red maples, and other scarlet autumn foliage found along this ridge and stream.

Schoolhouse Gap Kinzel Springs, TN se ❧ 1. Since there was probably never a school at this gap, the name may relate to the early days, when many of the children of Cades Cove and Whiteoak Sink passed through this gap en route to school in Townsend. 2. Another source, an elderly man, thinks he remembers a school near the gap.

Scott Gap, Scott Gap Branch, Scott Gap Cave Calderwood, TN/NC n ❧ Named for a George Scott family that lived in this area and cultivated land along Abrams Creek in pre-park days. (Note: a permit is required to enter all park caves.)

Scottish Mountain Cove Creek Gap, NC w ❧ Named for the Scottish Mountain Lumber Company that harvested timber in this area until park establishment. Formerly called Piney Butt.

Scratch Britches Mt. Le Conte, TN/NC w ❧ Named for an area thick enough with briers and thorns to rip one's pants.

Sea Branch Cades Cove, TN/NC n-ne ❧ 1. This name is probably a corruption of the name Seay, which is pronounced locally as "sea." The stream is probably named for a Seay family that once lived in this area. 2. Named for a lake or pond located northwest of the stream, and south of the south leg of the Cades Cove Loop Road.

Second Branch Gatlinburg, TN s-se ❧ Named for this stream's position between First Branch and Third Branch. All three streams are tributaries of Little River.

Seng Patch Branch Silers Bald, NC/TN nw ❧ This name is derived from the second syllable of the word ginseng (*Panax quinquefolium*). This attractive flowering plant was once harvested from the wilds of the Smokies, dried, and sold to local merchants, mostly for export to China. The Chinese name for the plant is Jin-chen, which means man-like and refers to the shape of its roots. The term patch refers to a natural bed of the plants growing close together. Sometimes also called sang. Digging ginseng has caused the plant to become uncommon in the Smokies. It is illegal to harvest ginseng in the national park today.

Sequoyah Branch Mt. Guyot, TN/NC m-e **Sequoyah Cemetery** Bunches Bald, NC w *n.s.* ❧ Named for Cherokee Chief Sequoyah or Sikwayi (1760-1843), a half white and half Cherokee whose German name was George Gist. His father was Nathaniel Gist and his mother Wureth, daughter of Cherokee Chief Old Tassel. He was inventor of a written Cherokee language (a syllabary) in 1821 and founder of the *Phoenix*, a Cherokee-English language newspaper. No other person in history is known to have invented an entire written language. He was never formally educated, nor did he read or write English or any language other than the one he invented.

Service Ridge Dellwood, NC w ❧ Probably named for the serviceberry (*Amelanchier* sp.), a small but common tree in the Smokies. It produces red berries that were often used to decorate churches during revival services. Called sarvis in the mountain vernacular.

Sevier County, Tennessee ❧ Named for John Sevier, first governor of Tennessee, 1794.

Shanty Branch Luftee Knob, NC/TN se **Shanty Mountain** Bunches Bald, NC ne ❧ Named for Old Smart, an African-American man who built a shanty (shack) on this stream and herded cattle on Shanty Mountain for a nearby land owner, Mitchell Davidson.

Sharptop Gap Hartford, TN/NC se ❧ Sharptop (a name referring to the abrupt peak of this mountain) is a former name for Mount Cammerer. The mountain's name has changed, but the gap's name has remained the same.

Shawano Ridge Luftee Knob, NC/TN w-sw-m-s ❧ Named for a tribe of Native Americans (possibly Shawnee) who once stopped on this ridge to make arrowheads prior to raiding a Cherokee settlement on the Oconaluftee River.

Shaw Grave Gap Calderwood, TN/NC s ❧ Named for the grave of a Union soldier by the name of Bas Shaw who was killed by North Carolina raiders and buried here near Deals Gap.

Sheep Pen Gap Cades Cove, TN/NC sw ❧ Sheep were grazed on nearby Gregory Bald and each fall they were herded into a large enclosure (a sheep pen) at this gap in preparation for the drive down to winter pasture, slaughter, or market. See also Lawson Gant Lot.

Shell Branch Kinzel Springs, TN s-sw ❧ Probably named for a Shell family that once lived along this stream.

Shehan Branch Tuskeegee, NC nw **Shehan Gap** Fontana Dam, NC ne ***n.s.*** ❧ Named for the Shehan family that settled in the Hazel Creek area in the late 1800s.

Shelter Branch Cades Cove, TN/NC se ❧ May have been named for a rock shelter in the area, or a man-made shelter, since its former name was Board Camp Branch (see Board Camp Gap).

Shields Branch Gatlinburg, TN sw ❧ Named for the Shields family that settled in the Cades Cove area in the 1830s.

Shootly Branch Calderwood, TN/NC w-m-nw ❧ Name is probably a corruption of Shottly, a family that once lived in the area.

Shop Creek Calderwood, TN/NC sw-w **Shop Ridge** Calderwood, TN/NC sw-w-m ❧ Allegedly named for an early settlement of Indian arrow makers who quarried their flint at or near Flint Gap on the Hannah Mountain Trail. Also see Flint Gap.

Shot Beech Ridge Clingmans Dome, NC/TN e-ne-n-m ❧ Named for an old beech tree (see Beech Gap) that once grew on this ridge. It was a favorite target for local hunters and had the gunshot scars to prove it.

Shuckstack Fontana Dam, NC n **Shuckstack Ridge** Fontana Dam, NC n-ne ❧ Named for this peak's resemblance to bunches of corn stalks stacked vertically in farm fields at harvest time. Also see Fodderstack Branch.

Shut-in Creek Thunderhead Mt., NC/TN n-m ❧ Named for a deep narrow gorge that is difficult to enter except at its mouth. The stream was considered to be enclosed or shut in by the gorge.

Shutts Prong Mt. Le Conte, TN/NC se-e ❧ 1. May have been named for Philip Shults (rather than Shutts), an early settler in the Webb Creek Valley area. He received a land grant here in 1841.
2. May also have been named for Perry M. Shultz who had a camp on Porters Creek and who once counterfeited silver half dollars in the area. This name has been spelled Shutts, Schultz, Schults, and Shults.

Silers Bald,* Silers Bald Spring Silers Bald, NC/TN m **Silers Creek, Silers Lead** Silers Bald, NC/TN n-m ❧ Named for Jesse Richardson Siler (1793–1876) who once owned and grazed livestock on this bald. *Previously called Big Stone Mountain. May have been the mythological Bald Mountain (U'tawagun'ta) of Cherokee legend.

Sinking Creek Luftee Knob, NC/TN w-nw ❧ So named because this stream sinks and flows beneath the surface rock, soil, logs, and brush debris that has accumulated along its course.

Sinks, The Wear Cove, TN e ✦ Named for deep pools below the falls where the stream bed has sunk down to a lower elevation. This is an excellent example of topographic "stream piracy" where a horseshoe-shaped stream meander has eroded through hard rock to create a new, steeper gradient river bed, leaving the old one high and dry. In this case, however, the process was not natural. During the great flood of 1896, about 900 logs being floated down the Little River to the saw mill were caught in a massive log jam at this site. This blockage diverted water across the neck

The Sinks

of the curve of the stream, thus creating a major problem for the England Lumber Company as logs continued to hang up here. To eliminate the problem, they drilled holes in the rocks, filled them with dynamite, and blew out a new stream channel. The jagged (rather than rounded) rocks at the Sinks today attest to this new stream location. As the water drops into the plunge pools of the falls, it swirls, not unlike water going down the drain of a sink.

Skidder Branch Bunches Bald, NC nw ❧ Probably named for a type of heavy machinery used in logging. Skidders were used in the Smokies to move logs from the woods to railroad sidings where they were loaded onto trains and delivered to saw mills. Such a device was probably employed along this stream in pre-park days.

Skunk Branch Calderwood, TN/NC n-w ***n.l.*** **Skunk Ridge** Calderwood, TN/NC sw-m-s-w ❧ Named for either the striped skunk (*Mephitis mephitis*) or the spotted skunk (*Spilogale putorius*), both of which are indigenous to the park. Skunks are sometimes called polecats by mountain folk.

Slab Camp Branch Silers Bald, NC/TN sw-s **Slab Cove, Slab Creek, Slab Creek Falls** Noland Creek, NC ne ❧ Named for bark slabs, the discarded, outside portions of logs that were trimmed off at sawmills. These slabs were often used in rustic construction, such as for hunting cabins, logging camp buildings, and other temporary structures. This name probably refers to either piles of these slabs (at the site of an old sawmill) or to their use in construction at these locations.

Slaty Branch Calderwood, TN/NC m ❧ Named for the slate quarries established along this stream in 1886 by the Abram's Creek Roofing and Slate Company, and later the Tennessee Slate Company. They quarried purple, green, and black rock and transported it to market down Panther Creek and Abrams Creek. The slate was used for roofs in Knoxville and Chattanooga as well as for pool tables and chalkboards.

Slick Limb Branch Gatlinburg, TN sw ❧ Possibly named for the slippery elm (*Ulmus rubra*) a tree whose bark easily slides off due to a slippery inner layer. Small toy slide whistles were once made from the twigs and smaller limbs of this tree.

Slide Branch Luftee Knob, NC/TN w ❧ This name may relate to a land or debris slide that once occurred along this stream. Such slides are not uncommon in the park.

Slide Hollow Silers Bald, NC/TN n ❧ Timber slides were constructed in this area to move logs to the railroads during pre-park logging days.

Smokemont Mill

Smokemont,* Smokemont Baptist Church *n.l.*, Smokemont Campground Smokemont, NC m ❧ Name believed to be short for Smoky Mountains (see Great Smoky Mountains). It was a former lumber company village, abandoned with park establishment, around 1939. *Formerly called Bradleytown, for the Thomas Bradley family, early settlers in this area. Also later called Lufty, a nickname for the Oconaluftee River, an adjacent stream.

Snag Branch Jones Cove, TN s-se **Snag Mountain** Mt. Guyot, TN/NC n-ne **Snaggy Ridge** Thunderhead Mt., NC/TN m ***n.l.*** ❧ Probably named for dead or dying trees visible at these places, or for solitary trees left by lumber companies.

Snake Den Mountain Luftee Knob, NC/TN nw ❧ So named because a local man, Joseph Campbell, once discovered a den (or nest) of rattlesnakes at this location. Locals shunned the mountain thereafter.

Snakefeeder Branch Mt. Guyot, TN/NC nw ❧ Named for insects called snakefeeders, snake doctors, or dragon flies (suborder *Anisoptera*) that are abundant along this and other Smoky Mountain streams. The names snake doctor and snake feeder are based on the folk belief that these insects take care of snakes.

Snake Tongue Silers Bald, NC/TN e ➧ Probably named because, from the air, this twin branch looks like a snake's forked tongue.

Soak Ash Creek Mt. Guyot, TN/NC nw ➧ Named for the old-fashioned process of soaking the ashes from wood fires in water to make lye. The resulting mixture was boiled down (evaporated) to obtain the lye, a strong alkaline substance used in making soap, hominy, and grits (ground hominy). See also Ash Hopper Branch.

Soapstone Branch Fontana Dam, NC ne **Soapstone Gap** Tuskeegee, NC nw ➧ Named for the presence of steatite or pyrophyllite (commonly called soapstone) that is used commercially in the manufacture of talcum powder and other products. The rock feels slick and soapy to the touch.

Solola Valley Noland Creek, NC ne ➧ This name, once applied to the local settlement and post office in this area, is a corruption of the Cherokee term salali, which means squirrel. It is also a corruption of the name of a legendary Cherokee storyteller and metal worker. See also Salola Branch.

Uncle Dave Sparks

Sparks Lane Cades Cove, TN/NC n ➧ Named for a Sparks family that lived in Cades Cove. James Sparks, head of the clan, settled in this cove sometime prior to 1830. The road was probably constructed in the 1840s.

Spence Branch Wear Cove, TN sw **Spence Cabin Branch*** Thunderhead Mt., NC/TN w ➧ See Spence Field. *Named for a cabin used by early cattle and sheep herders and later by hunters and campers.

Spence Field Thunderhead Mt., NC/TN w ➧ Spence Field, the largest grassy bald in the park, was named for James Robert Spence, who cleared this area for cattle grazing in the 1830s. He lived there in the warm months and spent winters at his home in

Cades Cove. The clearing was once up to 100 acres in size. The surrounding forest has since reclaimed all but 30 acres. Also once called the Spence Cabin (area).

Spicewood Branch #1 Wear Cove, TN sw-s **Spicewood Branch #2** Thunderhead Mt., NC/TN se *n.s.* ❥ Named for the spicebush (*Lindera benzoin*), a deciduous shrub common in the Smokies. The leaves and twigs of this plant have a strong spicy aroma when crushed.

Splatter Branch Wear Cove, TN m ❥ So named because as it drops off a bluff onto Little River Road, this stream splashes both the cars and people near it, especially after periods of heavy precipitation. Furthermore, when the Little River Railroad ran along this route, passengers getting off at this stop would likewise get splattered.

Split Branch Silers Bald, NC/TN ne ❥ So named because this stream splits into two nearly parallel branches.

Springhouse Branch #1 Noland Creek, NC nw **Springhouse Branch #2** Silers Bald, NC/TN se ❥ Probably named for springhouses once located along these streams. Springhouses were rock or frame structures usually built over a spring to keep the family water supply clean. Springhouses also provided some cooling for short-term food storage in the days before modern refrigeration.

Springhouse

Spruce Double Cades Cove, TN/NC nw **Spruce Double Branch** Calderwood, TN/NC ne ❥ The word double is sometimes used to refer to a twin or split tree trunk, ridge, stream, or some other feature. In this case it refers to a ridge and an adjacent stream. The spruce part of the name, considering the lower elevation of the ridge, probably refers to the eastern hemlock tree (*Tsuga canadensis*).

Spruce Flats* Wear Cove, TN s **Spruce Flats Branch** Wear Cove, TN s-se **Spruce Flats Cemetery**** Mt. Le Conte, TN/NC w *n.s.* **Spruce Flats Falls** Wear Cove, TN s *n.s.* ❥ Named for the presence of eastern hemlock trees (*Tsuga canadensis*) that mountain people often

Spruce Flats Falls

refer to as spruce or spruce pine. The true (red) spruce is found at higher elevations (generally above 4,000 feet). Hemlocks are found at lower elevations. *This area has also been called Wildcat. **Also known as Giles-Reagan-Bales Cemetery.

Spruce Mountain Bunches Bald, NC n-ne
Spruce Mountain Ridge Bunches Bald, NC ne ❧ Named for the red spruce trees (*Picea rubra*) that grow in this area. The red spruce generally grows above 4,000 feet in elevation and is associated with the Fraser fir tree, another high elevation species.

Spud Town Branch Silers Bald, NC/TN ne-n ❧ This creek was originally called Spud Tongue Branch, named for a tanbark spud, a spade-like tool used to strip bark from hemlocks, chestnuts, and other species of trees. The harvested bark was used in the leather tanning industry. One tannery was located in Walland, just a few miles from the Townsend entrance of the park. See also Bark Camp Run.

Standing Rock Ford Clingmans Dome, NC/TN nw ***n.l.*** ❧ Named for a 25-foot-high rock slab which protrudes vertically from the ground 150 feet upslope from one of the places that Road Prong Trail fords Road Prong.

Stickbait Branch Calderwood, TN/NC e-ne ❧ Named for various species of caddisfly larvae (*Pycnopsyche* sp.) that construct elaborate protective cases (cocoons) around their bodies using sticks, rocks, and other stream materials. Mountain people often used these larvae as fish bait, and because of the sticks and other debris attached to them, they were called stickbait.

Stillhouse Branch #1 Cades Cove, TN/NC ne **Stillhouse Branch #2** Hartford, TN/NC sw **Stillhouse Hollow** Wear Cove, TN s ❧ Probably named for moonshine stills once located along these streams and in this hollow.

Stillwell Creek Bunches Bald, NC w-n-m ❧ Named for an early prominent family in the Oconaluftee region of what is now the park.

Moonshine still

Stocking Hollow Wear Cove, TN s ***n.s.*** ❧ A hunter once stopped in this hollow to warm his feet. He took off his shoes, hung his stockings to dry too near the fire, and fell asleep. When he awoke, he discovered that his stockings had caught fire and burned.

Storehouse Branch Tuskeegee, NC m-e ***n.s.*** ❧ Probably named for the presence of some sort of storage building once constructed along this stream.

Striped Hollow Silers Bald, NC/TN ne ❧ Judging from its former name, Striped Rock Hollow, this name probably relates to striated, layered, or striped rocks in the area.

Styx Branch Mt. Le Conte, TN/NC s ❧ Named for the river of hell in Greek mythology, a river encircling the lower world, over which

Charon ferried dead souls. It is probably not coincidental that it flows through an area called Huggins Hell. See also Huggins Hell.

Sugar Cove Jones Cove, TN se **Sugar Cove Branch*** Cades Cove, TN/NC m **Sugar Cove Prong** Thunderhead Mt., NC/TN nw **Sugar Cove Ridge** Cades Cove, TN/NC sw-w **Sugarland Mountain** Clingmans Dome, NC/TN nw **Sugarlands, The**** Gatlinburg, TN e-se **Sugar Orchard Branch** Gatlinburg, TN s **Sugartree Gap** Thunderhead Mt., NC/TN e ❥ Named for the presence of sugar maple (*Acer saccharum*) trees, that were tapped for sap to make maple syrup and sugar. *Also known as Becky Sugar Cove (branch), for Becky Cable, a prominent former resident of Cades Cove. **Formerly known as Forks of the River (community).

Sugarloaf Branch Gatlinburg, TN e-se ***n.l.*** ❥ Named for a hard, conical-shaped mass of crystallized sugar used in the old days. When a quantity of sugar was needed, one would merely scrape or break it off the sugar loaf.

Sugartree Licks Bunches Bald, NC e ❥ The term lick may refer to natural or artificial salt licks in this area. It could also refer to the fact that as sap seeped from a wound in the bark of a sugar maple, it would evaporate on the surface as a sweet residue.

Suli Knob Silers Bald, NC/TN m **Suli Ridge** Silers Bald, NC/TN s-m ❥ Suli is the Cherokee term for vulture or buzzard.

Sunkota Ridge Bryson City, NC n-ne ❥ This name comes from a corrupted Cherokee term for apple, since apple trees grew on this ridge.

Sunup Knob Luftee Knob, NC/TN n ❥ Probably named for fact that one can view the rising sun from this promontory.

Surry Fork Mt. Le Conte, TN/NC m ❥ Surry is a corrupted pronunciation of the name Sarah. Named for Sarah Bohanan who once lived on this stream.

Sutton Ridge Hartford, TN/NC sw-s ❧ Named for a Joseph Sutton family that settled in the Cosby area on land grant #29149, issued June 24, 1854.

Swain County, North Carolina ❧ Named for David Lowry Swain (1801–1868). He was the Governor of North Carolina from 1832 to 1835, and later President of the University of North Carolina (1835–1868). Bryson City is the county seat.

Swallow Fork, Swallow Fork Trail Luftee Knob, NC/TN e-ne *n.l.* ❧ Probably named for the swift-flying, insect-eating birds common in this area.

Sweat Heifer Creek Clingmans Dome, NC/TN ne ❧ This name goes back to a time when cattle (including young, virgin female cows called heifers) were driven up the strenuous pathway along this stream to summer pasture. Any Sweat Heifer Creek Trail hiker can attest to the sweat factor involved in such a trek.

Sweet Branch Fontana Dam, NC n-m **Sweet Creek** Clingmans Dome, NC/TN nw ❧ 1. This name may be descriptive of the good water quality of these streams. 2. This name might also allude to the sugar maples along these streams that were once tapped for their sap to make maple syrup and sugar. 3. The name may refer to good moonshine making water. The old-timers say that you can't use just any water to make good moonshine. 4. See Sweet Gum Branch.

Sweet Gum Branch Calderwood, TN/NC se ❧ Named for the sweetgum trees (*Liquidambar styraciflua*) common along this stream. The name for the tree comes from the old-fashioned practice of using its sap as chewing gum.

Sweet Ridge Clingmans Dome, NC/TN nw ❧ Probably named for the sugar maple trees in this area (see Sugarland Mountain).

Tabcat Creek Calderwood, TN/NC sw-s ❧ Probably named for the bobcat (*Lynx rufus*) that has tabby (gray or brown) spots or stripes on its fur. Several older informants recall hearing bobcats referred to as tab cats.

Table Rock Branch Luftee Knob, NC/TN sw ❧ Possibly named for a flat rock formation along this stream.

Tabor Branch Smokemont, NC n-nw ❧ Probably named for a Tabor family that once lived in this area. A tabor is also a stronghold or fortified camp and a type of drum.

Takassah Ridge Silers Bald, NC/TN m-e ❧ Takassah is the Cherokee term for the eastern box turtle (*Terrapene carolina*).

Tali Gap Thunderhead Mt., NC/TN sw-s ❧ 1. This is the Cherokee term for the number two and it is probably not coincidental that the former name of this place was Double Gap. 2. May also be named for a Cherokee Indian from Wills Town who, along with other Cherokees and Creeks, attacked and killed three pioneers and wounded another on Crooked Creek, a branch of the Little River.

Tanager Branch Gatlinburg, TN w ❧ Named for the scarlet or summer tanager, bright red birds that spend their summers in the lower elevations of the Smoky Mountains.

Tarkiln Branch, Tarkiln Gap, Tarkiln Ridge Calderwood, TN/NC w-m ❧ Named for an early industry in this area in which tar and pitch were extracted from pine logs and stumps. The process involved slowly burning the wood in a circular, haystack-shaped, earthen structure called a tarkiln. The resulting hot liquid was caught down slope and further processed.

Tater Branch Cades Cove, TN/NC nw-n ❧ Named for a potato (tater in mountain vernacular) patch that some pioneer family planted along this stream.

Tater Ridge Cades Cove, TN/NC n ❧ This ridge is shaped like a potato (tater in mountain vernacular). It is thought to be a place where a young Indian woman jumped to her death when settlers killed her lover and where soldiers hid gold during the Civil War.

Taweesky Branch Thunderhead Mt., NC/TN sw ***n.s.*** ❧ Named for the Cherokee terms tawiska or tawiskage, meaning smooth or slick.

Taywa Creek Smokemont, NC n ❧ Taywa is the Cherokee term for flying squirrel.

Tea Branch Mt. Guyot, TN/NC n ***n.l.*** ❧ May be named for the teaberry plant (*Gaultheria procumbens*), a source of wintergreen flavoring. It is locally called mountain tea.

Thermo Branch, Thermo Knob Luftee Knob, NC/TN w ❧ Originally named Thermometer Knob by Arnold Guyot (see Mount Guyot) after he broke his thermometer on this peak while taking barometric pressure readings to determine its altitude. The name was later shortened to Thermo Knob.

Third Branch Gatlinburg, TN s ❧ Named for its location in respect to First and Second branches, which are also tributaries of Little River.

Thirst Branch Gatlinburg, TN e ❧ May be so named because this stream is sometimes dry (formerly named Dry Branch) and hence it could not always quench one's thirst.

Thomas Divide *n.l.*, Thomas Ridge Bryson City, NC ne ❧ Named for Col. William Holland Thomas, friend and ally to the Cherokee and called Wil-Usdi by them. He was a land speculator who commanded the Cherokee troops who joined the Confederate Army during the Civil War. Because the Cherokee could not, by law, purchase or own land at the time, he purchased 50,000 acres for them. This became the nucleus of the Qualla Boundary or Reservation, home of the Eastern Band of the Cherokee. He was also active in development of the road across Indian Gap. Thomas was adopted by the Cherokee tribe and with the death of Chief Yonaguska in 1839, he became a chief. Thomas was an attorney, entrepreneur, railroad promoter, and he served from 1848 to 1861 as a North Carolina State Senator.

Three Beech Fork Mt. Le Conte, TN/NC ne ***n.l.*** ❧ Probably named for three prominent American beech (*Fagus grandifolia*) trees (see Beech Gap) along this stream.

Three Forks (of Raven Fork) Mt. Guyot, TN/NC se ❧ This name refers to a place at the headwaters of Raven Fork. Looking upstream, the branch to the left is Left Fork #2, the one to the right is Right Fork, and the one in the center is Middle Fork.

Threetop Mountain Hartford, TN/NC sw ❧ This mountain was probably named for three mountain peaks in a row, one on either side of it. The north peak is Round Mountain, the center is Threetop Mountain, and the south peak is unnamed.

Moonshine still showing thumping chest

Thumper Branch Luftee Knob, NC/TN sw-s ❧ This name suggests former moonshining activity along this stream. In fact, the stream's earlier name was Stillhouse Branch (see Stillhouse Branch #1). The thumping chest (thumper and thump barrel) is part of a moonshine distilling apparatus and is located between the boiler and the condenser.

Thunderhead Mountain Thunderhead Mt., NC/TN m-w **Thunderhead Prong** Thunderhead Mt., NC/TN m-n **Thunderhead Spring** Thunderhead Mt., NC/TN m ❧ No one knows for sure how Thunderhead got its name. Perhaps it was due to its resemblance to a thunder cloud or a thunderhead. Maybe it was named for the numerous lightning strikes that occur along its crest. Cherokees called it Atagahi, meaning (oak) gall place, for the presence of many oak galls there.

Thunderhead Mountain from Cades Cove

Timothy Creek Jones Cove, TN sw ❧ Probably named for Timothy Reagan who once lived in this area.

Tipton Sugar Cove, Tipton Sugar Cove Branch Cades Cove, TN/NC w ❧ Named for the family of William (Fighting Billy) Tipton, a veteran of the American Revolution who received a land grant to settle in Cades Cove on March 23, 1821. His was the first family to legally settle in Cades Cove. See also Sugar Cove.

Titmouse Branch Cades Cove, TN/NC w ❧ Named for a small bird called the Tufted Titmouse (*Parus bicolor*).

Tobes Creek Hartford, TN/NC se ❧ Named for Tobias (Uncle Tobe) Phillips, a famed bear hunter and keeper of the toll gate on the Cataloochee Turnpike around the time of the Civil War.

Tollgate Branch Tapoco, NC/TN n *n.l.* ❧ Probably so named because a tollgate was once located here, where the toll road (now U.S. Highway 129) crossed this stream.

Tomahawk Prong Clingmans Dome, NC/TN nw ❧ Named for an Indian weapon that has a stone axe-like head and a wooden handle. Tomahawk is an Algonquin term. Perhaps such an artifact was once found along this stream. Otherwise, it is related in theme to nearby Indian Grave Flats and Moccasin Branch.

Tom Branch, Tom Branch Falls Bryson City, NC n ❧ Probably named for Tom Wiggins, a former Confederate soldier who lived in a house and operated a grist mill on this stream from 1854 to 1892.

Toms Creek Hartford, TN/NC sw-s ❧ Named for Tom Holland, a former resident of this area. According to one source, he and his brother John used to go hunting in the same general area, but would follow parallel creeks to their common source, a spring. John's creek is not labeled on the topographic map. A second stream is shown running parallel to Toms Creek, but there is no common source (shown) for the two streams.

Tooni Branch Bunches Bald, NC w ❧ This stream is probably named for a Cherokee family that lived in the area. Also spelled Tuni.

Tower Creek Smokemont, NC ne *n.l.* ❧ Probably named for a Tower family that once lived in this area.

Colonel W.B. Townsend

Townsend Y (or Wye) Wear Cove, TN s-sw *n.l.* ❧ So named because the Left and Middle Prongs of Little River come together here in the shape of a Y. Townsend is a community just northwest of the Y. It is named for Colonel Wilson B. Townsend who established the Little River Lumber Company in the Smokies in 1902. The community was formerly called Tuckaleechee, after the large cove in which it is located.

Tow String Creek Smokemont, NC s-se-e ❧ 1. Named for the tow string, a yarn made of course broken flax or hemp fibers. It was reported that an old woman once made tow string here and sold it to settlers. 2. Named for an old Indian by the name of Tow. 3. Some men who lived along this stream wore tow pants made from tow yarn material. One day, while they were hunting ginseng, their pants got wet and shrunk up to their knees. After that, some locals started calling this Tow String Creek.

Tremont Thunderhead Mt., NC/TN n ❧ When the Little River Lumber Company developed a camp at the confluence of Thunderhead Prong and Lynn Camp Prong, and established a hotel and post office there, they had to have a name for the town. Their first choice was Walkers Valley, in honor of the famed Walker family that settled the area. Unfortunately, that name was already taken. So, in the spirit of the names of nearby Elkmont (and the more distant Smokemont), they decided on the name Tremont for the abundance of trees in these mountains. Formerly called Walkers Valley, Lost Cove, and Tar Paper Camp.

Tri Corner Knob,* Tri Corner Knob Spring Mt. Guyot, TN/NC e ❧ Named for the shape of this ridge, which resembles a tri-corner hat, popular in Revolutionary War times. Three counties—Sevier County, Tennessee; Haywood County, North Carolina; and, at the time, Jackson (now Swain) County, North Carolina, also came together here along the state line ridge. This is also the intersection of Balsam Mountain (the park's largest transverse ridge) and the main crest of the Smokies, forming a three ridge intersection. This area was named by geographer A. Guyot (see Mount Guyot) prior to 1860. *At an elevation of 6,120 feet above sea level, this is the eleventh highest free-standing peak in the park.

Trillium Branch Mt. Le Conte, TN/NC e-m **Trillium Gap*** Mt. Le Conte, TN/NC m ❧ Named for the abundance of trillium (*Trillium* sp.) flowers at these locations. The plants are called trillium because their leaves and other flower parts are in three's or multiples of three. *This name was suggested by former National Park Service director Horace Albright, after seeing the profuse growth of these flowers at this gap. Formerly called Brushy Gap and Grassy Gap.

Trout Branch Mt. Le Conte, TN/NC sw-s ❧ Named for the fish of which there are three species in the park; the brook trout (*Salvelinus fontinalis*), the rainbow trout (*Salmo gairdneri*), and the brown trout (*Salmo trutta*). Only the brook trout is native.

Tub Mill Creek Cades Cove, TN/NC se-e ❧ Named for the presence of a tub or turbine grist mill on this stream. A turbine mill has horizontal wheels and vanes that are turned by fast-running water to grind cornmeal and flour. Small tub mills were once numerous throughout the Smokies. Some say they were called tub mills because they could only grind about a tub of meal per day.

Tuckaseegee River Bryson City, NC w ❧ The original Cherokee name for this stream, Tsiksitsi, was later corrupted to Tuckaseegee. One source stated that the original meaning of the word is not known. Another says that the word means terrapin (a turtle). Also once called Tuckaseej River.

Tuliptree

Tulip Branch Gatlinburg, TN s ❧ Named for the very large tuliptrees, also called tulip poplars or yellow poplars, (*Liriodendron tulipifera*) found in this area prior to large scale logging operations. This stream was formerly called Poplar Branch for the same reason.

Tunnel Branch Noland Creek, NC m-e **Tunnel Ridge** Noland Creek, NC n-ne-e-m ❧ Legend has it that this ridge and branch were named for one or more early gold mine tunnels.

Turkey Flyup Clingmans Dome, NC/TN e ❧ So named because, according to the Indians, turkeys could always be found at this location by hunters.

Turkey Pen Branch Luftee Knob, NC/TN sw-s **Turkeypen Ridge** Cades Cove, TN/NC ne ❧ Named for turkey traps (called turkey pens) placed in the woods to catch these wily birds.

Turnback Branch Wear Cove, TN sw ❧ Probably named for a long bend in the railroad tracks that followed this stream. At one point, it was said, the curve was so sharp that you could look ahead and see the end of the train in which you were riding.

Turner Branch Wear Cove, TN s-se ❧ Named for George Turner, an African-American man who lived in the Rough Creek area and later moved (with a logging operation) to the Tremont area of the Smokies.

Tuskee Gap Smokemont, NC w ❧ Probably a shortened version of Tuskegee, which in the Creek Indian language means warriors.

Twentymile Cascade Fontana Dam, NC nw *n.s.* **Twentymile Creek** Cades Cove, TN/NC s-sw **Twentymile Ridge** Fontana Dam, NC n-nw ❧ 1. So named because it is twenty miles from the mouth of Twentymile Creek to the old town of Bushnell (now beneath the waters of Fontana Lake). 2. So named because the mouth of Twentymile Creek, which is now on Cheoah Lake, is twenty miles from the mouth of Hazel Creek, now on Fontana Lake.

Twin Creek Mt. Le Conte, TN/NC n-m ❧ Named for two streams that run parallel to one another for almost a mile and a half.

Twin Creeks Research Laboratory Gatlinburg, TN e ❧ Named for two parallel branches of Le Conte Creek. They run past this ecological research center near Gatlinburg, Tennessee.

Twin Falls Mt. Le Conte, TN/NC m ❧ Named for a 150-foot double waterfall that flows into Roaring Fork.

Twomile Branch Gatlinburg, TN e ❧ 1. May be so named because this stream flows into the West Prong of the Little Pigeon River approximately two miles southwest of the original center of the town of Gatlinburg. 2. The name could describe the stream's length, although it is actually 2.5 miles long.

Twomile Lead Gatlinburg, TN e ❧ So named because this ridge is approximately two miles long. See glossary for term lead.

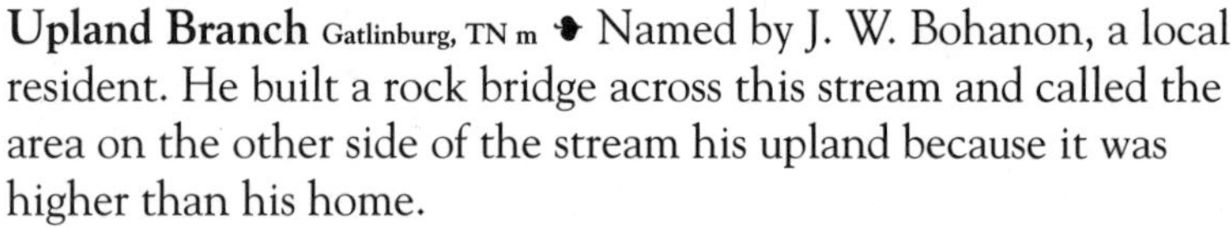

Upland Branch Gatlinburg, TN m ❧ Named by J. W. Bohanon, a local resident. He built a rock bridge across this stream and called the area on the other side of the stream his upland because it was higher than his home.

Vee Hollow Branch Wear Cove, TN m ❧ Probably named for the shape of this hollow, which is narrow at the bottom and broad at the top. See glossary for term hollow.

Veery Branch Thunderhead Mt., NC/TN m *n.s.* ❧ Probably named for the Veery (*Catharus fuscescens*), a common bird above 3,500 feet in the Smokies.

Victory Branch Cades Cove, TN/NC nw ❧ Believed to be named for a metal commemorative band or ring protruding from a tree that has grown around it. This makeshift monument has the Armistice date, November 11, 1918, inscribed on it. It marks the United States (Allied) victory and the end of World War I. The tree is said to be located somewhere along the bank of this stream.

Walker Camp Prong Clingmans Dome, NC/TN n ❧ Named for a Walker family, early settlers in this area that may have had a hunting or fishing camp along this stream.

Walker Fields Wear Cove, TN s ❧ Named for William Marion (Black Bill or Big Bill) Walker who settled in this area with his wife Nancy Caylor in 1859. He was the father of three legitimate and at least 17 illegitimate children.

Black Bill and Nancy Walker

Walkers Creek Thunderhead Mt., NC/TN se-e ❧ Named for a Walker family that originally settled in the Hazel Creek area in the late 1800s.

Walker Sisters Cabin Wear Cove, TN e ❧ Named for the five spinster daughters of John N. Walker, whose wife Margaret Jane Walker bore 11 children in this cove. See Five Sisters Cove. Also known as the King-Walker cabin for Wiley King who owned the land and built the cabin in the 1850s. King's son-in-law, John Walker, acquired the land and enlarged and renovated the cabin around 1865.

Walnut Bottom Luftee Knob, NC/TN n-ne ❧ Probably named for the black walnut trees (*Juglans nigra*) that grow in this area.

War Branch Silers Bald, NC/TN n ❧ See Battle Branch.

Wash Ridge Bunches Bald, NC ne ❧ 1. Wash was often a nickname for a person whose first name was Washington. Naming a child after George Washington was a common practice in the old days. This may be the origin of this place name, although which Washington it refers to is not known. 2. Name may also refer to a natural wash or erosion area on this ridge.

Wasulu Ridge Tuskeegee, NC ne ❧ This is the Cherokee term for a large, red-brown moth that can be seen around blooming tobacco plants. Tobacco may have been cultivated along this stream at one time.

Watercrease Branch Mt. Le Conte, TN/NC w ❧ Named for a small, edible, perennial plant (*Nasturtium officinale*) that is a member of the mustard family. It grows in springs and slow streams and has a mild pungent flavor. Mountain people often called it watercrease or just crease, but others know it as water cress. This name could also refer to mountain watercress, spring cress, or Pennsylvania bitter cress.

Waterdog Branch Gatlinburg, TN sw-s ❧ Named for the waterdog (*Necturus maculosus*), a large aquatic salamander found in some streams at the lower elevations. Also sometimes called a mudpuppy.

Water Oak Gap Silers Bald, NC/TN sw ❧ Since the true water oak (*Quercus nigra*) does not occur in the park, the gap is probably named for a similar species, possibly the southern red oak (*Quercus falcata*).

Water Tank Branch Wear Cove, TN se ❧ Probably named for a railroad water tank that once stood along this stream, or for the fact that the railroad used this stream as a source of water for its steam locomotives.

Watson Cove Clingmans Dome, NC/TN s ❧ Probably named for a Watson family, early settlers in the Gatlinburg area.

Wear Cove Gap Wear Cove, TN e ❧ Named for Wear Cove, which had earlier been named for Col. Samuel Wear, a pioneer who settled along the West Fork of Little Pigeon River at Waldens

Creek. Wear built a fort here for protection of his family and neighbors against the Cherokee and Creek Indians. This was vital since the Great Indian War Path of the Creeks crossed his land. He was one of the best known and most influential men in Sevier County's early history. Col. Wear played a role in the development of the Territory South of the River Ohio (under Governor William Blount), the failed state of Franklin, and the state of Tennessee. He was the first Clerk of Sevier County, and he served in the militia under John Sevier (see Sevier County), the first governor of Tennessee. Wear settled his namesake valley in 1795, on land acquired as a Revolutionary War land grant. Formerly called Grassy Gap. Wear Cove was originally called Crowson Cove, for Aaron Crowson, believed to have been its first settler.

Weasel Branch Calderwood, TN/NC e ❥ Named for the long-tailed weasel (*Mustela frenata*) or least weasel (*Mustela nivalis*) both of which live in the Great Smoky Mountains.

Long-tailed weasel

Weaver Creek Mt. Guyot, TN/NC s-se ***n.l.*** ❥ Probably named for a Weaver family that once lived in this area.

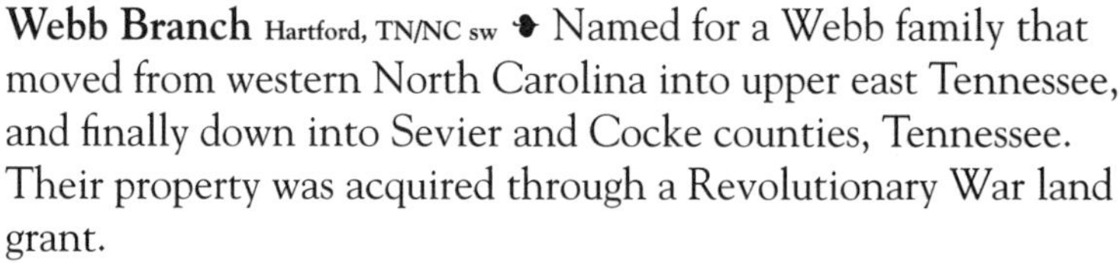

Webb Branch Hartford, TN/NC sw ❥ Named for a Webb family that moved from western North Carolina into upper east Tennessee, and finally down into Sevier and Cocke counties, Tennessee. Their property was acquired through a Revolutionary War land grant.

Webb Creek Jones Cove, TN s **Webb Overlook** Clingmans Dome, NC/TN w ❥ Named in honor of Charles A. Webb (1866–1949) an attorney, teacher, legislator, U.S. Marshall, and owner-publisher of the Asheville *Citizen-Times*. Webb participated in the 1899 meeting that launched the first organized effort to establish a national park in the Appalachians. He served as a member and eventually vice chairman of the Appalachian National Park Association, which negotiated the land acquisitions on the North Carolina side of the park. His newspaper was instrumental in supporting North Carolina's efforts to raise the $2 million that was matched by the Rockefellers (see Rockefeller Memorial). He was also instrumental in establishing Mt. Mitchell State Park and the Blue Ridge Parkway in North Carolina.

Wedge Ridge Blockhouse, TN se ➧ Thought to be named for its shape. From a distance, it looks like a wedge between two ridges.

Welch Bald Tuskeegee, NC ne **Welch Branch #1*** Noland Creek, NC n **Welch Branch #2** Noland Creek, NC w **Welch Ridge** Noland Creek, NC ne ➧ These areas were named for 1. A Washington Welch family that settled in this area of the Smokies circa 1852. 2. A Major William A. Welch. 3. A Dr. Robert V. Welch, a prominent physician who had part interest in the land in this area. Such individuals were known as land speculators. *Probably named for a Welch family that settled in the Forney Creek area in the early 1800s.

West Point Mt. Le Conte, TN/NC s ➧ Named for a westerly peak of Mount Le Conte. Also see Mount Le Conte.

Wet Bottom Trail Cades Cove, TN/NC nw ***n.s.*** ➧ So named because it runs through the poorly drained floodplain of Abrams Creek, and is often very muddy, especially after heavy precipitation. See glossary for term bottom.

Whaley Cemetery Mt. Le Conte, TN-NC e ***n.s.*** **Whaley, Elijah Cemetery** Mt. Le Conte, TN/NC ne ➧ Named for a Whaley family, the first settlers in the Greenbrier Cove area.

Whim Knob Bunches Bald, NC e ➧ So named because a whim (a winch or pulley utilizing horse power) was used on this peak to pull logs down the valley during timber cutting operations.

Whistlepig Branch Gatlinburg, TN m ➧ See Groundhog Creek. Formerly called Sol Branch. In this case, sol could mean sun or it could be the first name of a boy or man, surname unknown.

Whistling Branch Cades Cove, TN/NC m-n **Whistling Gap** Cades Cove, TN/NC m ❥ Name may have been associated with a whistle punk or bell boy, a device used by the logging industry to provide whistle signals on a log skidder.

White Mans Glory Creek Silers Bald, NC/TN sw-s ❥ See Mount Glory.

Whiteoak Branch Noland Creek, NC n **Whiteoak Flats Branch** Wear Cove, TN s **White Oak Mountain** Cove Creek Gap, NC s-m **Whiteoak Ridge** Noland Creek, NC n ❥ Named for the white oak trees (*Quercus alba*) in these areas.

Whiteoak Sink Kinzel Springs, TN se ❥ A large sinkhole (see glossary) near Cades Cove, named for white oak trees (*Quercus alba*) which are not as numerous now as they were before a large portion of the sink area was cultivated by early settlers.

Whiteside Creek Tuskeegee, NC w-m-n ❥ The name Whiteside may be a corruption of wayside since this stream was along a portion of the old route to Wayside, North Carolina. Today, some locals call it Millsaps Creek, after J. C. (Jess) Millsaps who once lived there.

White Walnut Branch Thunderhead Mt., NC/TN s ❥ Probably named for the butternut or white walnut trees (*Juglans cinerea*) found in this area. Butternuts are infrequent trees in the park and are declining due to a fungus infestation.

Wildcat Branch #1 Cades Cove, TN/NC w-m **Wildcat Branch #2** Thunderhead Mt., NC/TN se **Wildcat Knob*** Hartford, TN/NC sw ❥ Probably named for the mountain lion or panther (*Felis concolor*) that many mountain people call a wildcat.

Wild Cherry Branch Clingmans Dome, NC/TN ne **Wild Cherry Ridge** Silers Bald, NC/TN e ❧ Probably named for numerous wild cherry trees (*Prunus* sp.) growing at these sites. Such stands are sometimes indicative of burned-over land. A particular species called fire or pin cherry (*Prunus pensylvanica*) is often found in almost pure stands in burned-over areas.

Wildham Community Calderwood, TN/NC w *n.s.* ❧ Named for an old community, which in turn was probably named for a family that once lived there.

Wilson Branch Cades Cove, TN/NC nw ❧ Named for a Wilson family that settled in Cades Cove in the 1870s or 1880s.

Winding Stair Branch Cove Creek Gap, NC s ❧ Name is probably descriptive of the way this branch crisscrosses and meanders down its rocky stream bed like a winding staircase.

Wolf Cove Creek Bunches Bald, NC ne **Wolf Ridge*** Cades Cove, TN/NC sw ❧ Named for the gray wolf (*Canis lupus*) that was extirpated from the Smokies in pioneer times. *Name derived from an incident involving a wolf that allegedly killed 20 sheep in one night on Gregory Bald. Russell Gregory and another local man, Andy Greer, tracked the wolf to a hollow log on this ridge, killed her, found 11 pups and killed them. Thereafter, this place was called Wolf Ridge.

Wonderland Hotel Gatlinburg, TN sw *n.l.* ❧ Named for the Wonderland Park Company that opened a hotel here in 1912 to serve logging company employees. Later it became a private club, called the Wonderland Club. With park establishment, it opened its doors to tourists as the Wonderland Hotel. It finally closed in 1992. The name fittingly describes the area as a land of wonders. See also Elkmont.

Wonderland Hotel

Woodchuck Branch Thunderhead Mt., NC/TN ne ❧ Probably named for the woodchuck (*Marmota monax*), a large and stocky member of the rodent family, also know as groundhog or whistlepig.

Woodward Knob Thunderhead Mt., NC/TN sw ❧ Probably named for a family that once lived in this area. May also be a corruption of Woodard rather than Woodward, as there were Woodards living in the general area.

Woody Branch Cove Creek Gap, NC w **Woody Creek*** Bunches Bald, NC n-ne **Woody Ridge** Bunches Bald, NC n-ne ❧ Probably named for Woody families who lived in these areas. *Probably named for an S. L. or Jonathan Woody family that settled in the Cataloochee area. Formerly called Straight Creek because its course was straight for almost four miles.

Stephen and Mary Woody

Woolly Ridge, Woolly Ridge Branch Thunderhead Mt., NC/TN m-s **Woolly Tops Branch** Mt. Guyot, TN/NC w **Woolly Tops Mountain**

Mt. Guyot, TN/NC w-m ❧ Mountain folk described places covered with dense thickets of rhododendron or mountain laurel as woolly.

Yanu Branch, Yanu Ridge Silers Bald, NC/TN s ❧ Yanu is the Cherokee term for bear.

Yellow Branch Mt. Guyot, TN/NC se *n.l.* **Yellow Creek** Luftee Knob, NC/TN nw-n **Yellow Creek Gap** Luftee Knob, NC/TN nw ❧ May be named for the presence of yellow autumn foliage (such as is found on tuliptrees and sugar maples).

GLOSSARY

Apiary—A place where bee hives (or bee gums) are kept for the harvesting of honey.

Arm—A colloquial term for a ridge or a spur of a ridge or mountain.

Bald—A treeless area found on a mountain summit, ridge, gap, or slope. Some are natural and some were created by people and artificially maintained as pastures. Grassy balds are covered by grasses, sedges, and other herbaceous growth. Heath balds are dominated by shrubs and low growing woody vegetation, many of which belong to the heath (*Ericaceae*) family.

Balsam—A species of tree as well as a high altitude area where firs are the dominant tree species. Such areas often appear dark or even black from a distance.

Bench—A broad ledge or level area along the flank of a ridge or mountain.

Bottom(s)—Relatively flat terrain, particularly along a stream. The low, well-drained, bottom land soils are often fertile and productive, but can also be submerged by floodwater part of the year, and be nonproductive. Also defined as level alluvial land.

Branch—A tributary of a larger stream, usually considered smaller than a creek or brook.

Brook—A small stream, generally smaller than a creek.

Butt—The abrupt, broken-off end of a ridge or mountain. A promontory or headland. A hillock or mound. A short broad projection from the lower part of a mountain, possibly a coastal term carried inland.

Butte—A flat-topped, steep-walled hill, usually standing alone.

Cascade—A series of waterfalls flowing over steep rock faces at a less than vertical gradient, as opposed to a free-fall of water.

Chasm—A deep cleft, fissure, or crack in the earth's surface. A break or a gap.

Cove—A relatively small, level-floored valley between ridges or mountains.

Creek—A small stream, somewhat larger than a brook and smaller than a river.

Deadening(s)—An area where pasture or farmland is created by killing large numbers of trees by girdling them (e.g., cutting them all the way around their bark to stop the flow of sap). The trees can then be chopped down for firewood the following year and their stumps and limbs either burned in place, dug out, or left to rot.

Den—The shelter or retreat of a wild animal; a lair. Also a cave or hollow used as a hiding place.

Divide—The ridges or regions of high ground that separate stream valleys.

Dome—A rounded mountain or ridge top.

Falls—A near vertical free-drop waterfall, as opposed to a cascade. Also known as a cataract.

Fire Scald—A barren or once-barren area in wooded terrain, caused by a fire.

Fittified Spring—An intermittent spring that is low or dry one minute and free flowing the next. Also called a spasmodic spring.

Flat(s)—Broad level areas along streams or surrounded by slopes.

Fork—A generic term designating a branch or a tributary of a stream or a branch or spur of an elevated landform such as a mountain or ridge.

Gap—A break in a mountain; a pass or cleft.

Glade—An open space in a forest; an area of clumped or sparse woody vegetation.

Glen—A narrow, secluded valley.

Gorge—A deep, narrow passage with steep rocky sides; a ravine.

Grassy Patches—Cultivated, or once-cultivated, stands of grass found in treeless areas. Grassy areas beneath trees, along streams, ridges, etc.

Gulf—A deep, wide valley, gorge, or hollow.

Heath Bald—Treeless areas on mountain tops, gaps, and the sides of ridges. They are covered with shrubby and herbaceous plants of the heath (*Ericaceae*) family, including rhododendron, mountain laurel, dog-hobble, sand myrtle, and others.

Hell—A place where the vegetation is so thick and tangled that one may not be able to penetrate it, or may get lost in it. A cut over, burned, and eroded landscape. Also see laurel hell.

High Top—A lofty peak.

Hog Back (Ridge)—A steep, sheer ridge top, often with sharp jutting rocks.

Hollow—A hollow, or "holler" in the vernacular of the mountain people, is a small valley between mountains.

Knob—A rounded hill or mountain. A knoll.

Knoll—A small rounded hill or mountain.

Laurel Bed—A dense, impenetrable thicket of mountain laurel or rhododendron.

Laurel Hell—An area of thick, tangled, and almost impenetrable vegetation, mostly mountain laurel, rhododendron, dog-hobble, or similar dense, shrubby growth. Said to be hell to navigate through, and a place in which only the Devil himself would feel comfortable. See also laurel slick.

Laurel Slick—Same as laurel hells, except when seen from a distance, they appear slick or smooth in comparison to other surrounding woody vegetation.

Lead—A long ridge or mountain usually extended from another ridge or mountain. May also connect two ridges or mountains.

Lick—Also called a salt or mineral lick. A deposit of exposed natural (or artificial) mineral salt that is licked by passing animals. Salt is necessary in the diets of animals such as deer and cattle.

New Ground—Land that has recently been cleared for cultivation or pasture.

Peak—The crest or summit of a hill or mountain.

Pinnacle—A tall, sometimes slender, pointed formation; an acute peak, ridge, or mountain.

Plunge Pool—A basin or pool of water at the base of a waterfall.

Point—A high, abrupt ridge or mountain peak.

Prong—A branch, fork, or tributary of a stream.

Range—A series of connected mountains, considered a single system.

Ridge—A natural raised part of the earth's surface, generally larger than a hill. A long, narrow elevation of land or a range of hills or mountains.

Run—A small swift stream, often fairly straight and on a steep gradient.

Saddle—A ridge between two high peaks or summits.

Sag—A low-lying area along a ridge or mountain top, not as pronounced as a gap.

Sinkhole—A depression in the ground, generally caused by the collapse of underlying caverns.

Shoals—Shallow places along a stream, sometimes with small falls or cascades.

Slick—See Laurel Slick.

Spring—A flow of water above ground level that occurs where the water table intercepts the ground surface.

Spur—A lateral ridge projecting from a mountain or mountain range.

Swag—A gap or depression along a ridge or mountain top, a sag.

Top—A summit, the top of a ridge, mountain, or bald.

Valley—A stretch of low-lying land, between hills or mountains, often with one or more streams flowing through it.

Woollies (Woolly Patches, Wooly-heads)—Another name for laurel hells and slicks.

ABOUT THE AUTHOR

Allen R. Coggins supports his passion for writing and historical research by working full time for the Oak Ridge Institute for Science and Education and part time with Personnel Technology Group, Inc., in Oak Ridge. He was born in Knoxville and he and his wife Barbara reside in Blount County in the shadow of their beloved Smokies. He has published well over 100 articles on topics ranging from conservation to humor and from natural science to disasters. He is presently researching Tennessee's greatest natural disasters.

RAVENS FORD 0.7
ROUND BOTTOM 12.0

RAVENS FORD 0.7
ROUND BOTTOM 12.0

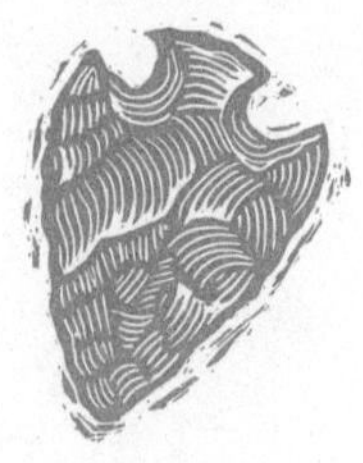

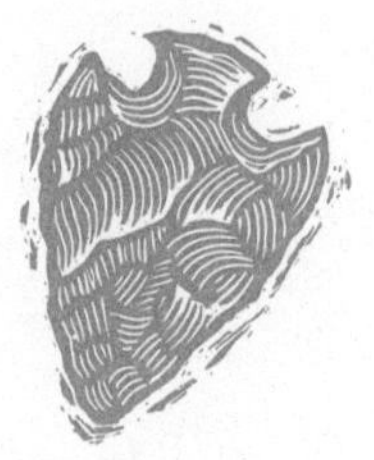

RAVENS FORD 0.7
ROUND BOTTOM 12.0